AMERICAN CLOCKS

A · N · D

CLOCKMAKERS

AMERICAN CLOCKS

A · N · D

CLOCKMAKERS

ROBERT W. & HARRIETT SWEDBERG

Wallace-Homestead Book Company
Radnor, Pennsylvania

Copyright © 1989 by Robert W. and Harriett Swedberg
All Rights Reserved
Published in Radnor, Pennsylvania 19089, by Wallace-Homestead Book Company

Designed by Anthony Jacobson
Photographs by the authors; printing and enlarging by Tom Luse
Manufactured in the United States of America

Library of Congress Cataloging-in-Publication Data

Swedberg, Robert W.
    American clocks and clockmakers.
    Bibliography: p. 175
    Includes index.
    1. Clocks and watches—United States—History.
2. Clocks and watches—United States—Collectors and
collecting—Catalogs. I. Swedberg, Harriett. II. Title.
TS543.U6S94   1989   681.1′13′0973   88-51500
ISBN 0-87069-525-8

2 3 4 5 6 7 8 9 0   8 7 6 5 4 3 2 1 0

To Tom Luse,
our indispensable photo developer, printer, and enlarger,
whose careful and painstaking workmanship over the past twelve years
has contributed greatly to the success of our books

Contents

Acknowledgments

The authors sincerely thank the following collectors and dealers who freely gave their time and knowledge to assist us in obtaining photographs for this book. We also thank those clock collectors who did not wish to be listed.

Antique Mall
Shafer & Sons Clock Co.
Jerry and Judy Shafer, NAWCC member,
    023604
Rockford, Illinois

Antique Scene
Rachel and Jack Cattrell
Moline, Illinois

Marion and Vera Blevins, NAWCC
    member

Gary Bowker

Richard and Norma Broline, NAWCC
    member, 025202

Butterworth Clock Repair
Mark Butterworth, NAWCC member,
    077581
Muscatine, Iowa

Chuck Cline, NAWCC member 060109

James Stanley Feehan
Joy, Illinois

Bennie L. Hack, NAWCC member
    039717
Decatur, Illinois

Jack Heisler, NAWCC member

Carmon M. and Peggy M. Howe,
    NAWCC member, 023577

The Illinois Antique Center
Dan and Kim Philips
Peoria, Illinois

Mort Jacobs Restorations, NAWCC
    member
Chicago, Illinois

The Louisville Antique Mall
Harold L., Chuck, and Don Sego
Louisville, Kentucky

Old Timers—Antique Clocks
Dick Masters, NAWCC member
Louisville Antique Mall
Louisville, Kentucky

The Oldest Son's Antiques and Appraisal
    Service
Nancy, Jerry, and helper Jason
Pocahontas, Illinois

Prairie Peddler
Gretchen and Terry Poffinbarger
Davenport, Iowa

Pritts Antiques, NAWCC member
Talvia and Theral
Decatur, Illinois

Smokehouse Square Antiques
Ken and Lesley Denzin
Amana, Iowa

Swedberg's Antiques
Bob and Harriett, NAWCC member
    097530
Antique Mall
Iowa City, Iowa

Cheryl Swedberg

John Tanner, NAWCC member
Chino, California

Village Square Antiques
Theresa and Glen Nance
Pocahontas, Illinois

Karen, Terry, Adam, and Cody Watson

1
Introduction to Collecting and Pricing Clocks

The prices in this book should be used only as a guide. They were set by the collectors, dealers, and NAWCC members whose clocks are pictured in this book. None of the prices has been set by the authors. As a consequence, neither the authors nor the publisher assumes responsibility for any losses that might incur as a result of consulting this guide.

Our books attempt to assist novices who seek to learn more about collectible and antique articles. We use no museum or catalogue pictures. Our photographs are all from private homes, shows, conventions, or shops.

Pricing is extremely subjective and price guides will not change this. One NAWCC member said that he could tell you the value of all his clocks, and if you went to another collector who had a similar collection of clocks, his prices would probably differ greatly—either in the lower or higher range.

Several examples of the vagaries of pricing will demonstrate this individuality.

In this chapter is a photograph of an Ansonia ebonized wall clock listed for $800. In the course of our research and travels we photographed two other identical clocks in two different states. One was priced at $500 and the other at $1,000. Certainly there cannot be any greater subjectivity in pricing than that.

Two identical Waterbury "Halifax" oak wall clocks are pictured in Chapter 4. The Illinois example is listed at $600, while its Iowa counterpart carries a price tag of $300.

Two miniature Seth Thomas OG shelf clocks, pictured in Chapter 3, differed by $150.

Another example of the extreme difference in pricing involves two identical Ansonia Brass & Copper Company "Novelty Calendar" octagon, short-drop, simple calendar clocks, pictured in Chapter 4—one with a $500 price tag and the other with a $1,000 tag.

One Ansonia "Queen Elizabeth" mahogany wall clock pictured in this chapter

Waterbury "Alton" oak wall clock; 8-day, time and strike, spring driven; 16" wide, 39" high, 7" dial; $600. Ansonia "Queen Elizabeth" mahogany wall clock; 8-day, time and strike, spring driven, 13½" wide, 37½" high, 7" dial; $900.

Ansonia reflector ebony-finished wall clock with Mary Gregory-type etching on tablet, circa 1880; 8-day, time and strike, spring driven; 14" wide, 35" high; $800.

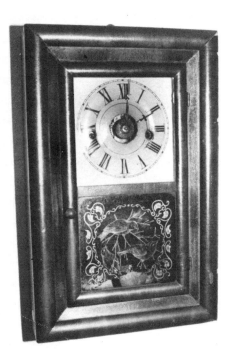

Seth Thomas miniature ogee mahogany veneered shelf clock with S and T on hands for Seth Thomas, after 1865; 30-hour, time, strike, and alarm; 10" wide, 16" high; $100.

*Seth Thomas miniature ogee mahogany shelf clock, after 1865; 8-day, time and strike; 10½" wide, 16½" high; **$175**. Seth Thomas miniature ogee mahogany-veneered shelf clock with S and T on hands for Seth Thomas, after 1865; 30-hour, time and strike, 10" wide, 16" high; **$225**.*

is priced at $900. Another such clock, but made of oak and pictured in the color section, was found in another state and priced at $800. These examples can be multiplied many times as you look at the clocks and prices in this book. We're sure your subjectivity will elicit comments similar to "That's too high," or "That's too low," as you compare the clocks and their prices.

Some of the NAWCC members who helped us in developing this book did not wish to be acknowledged, while others did not wish to put prices on some of their clocks—particularly those clocks in the hard-to-find and unusual category. We honored both requests.

As you search for clocks, use caution because many clocks for sale, particularly at some large auctions, are "marriages"— the parts from several clocks being used to make one clock. Countless NAWCC members told us that some dealers and merchants prepare for months at a time getting such clocks ready for the unsuspecting novice buyer.

Buy from a reputable dealer, one to whom you may return your purchase if it does not meet the standards that have been established for it.

We have attempted to check and recheck the information we have used in this book, but we have found that even among the established authorities in the field, they too sometimes disagree regarding dates, founders, and names. One calendar-clock inventor, Maranville, is listed with two different first names—Alusha and Galusha. Kroeber, too, is listed as Francis or Florence, depending on which source you read. One source lists Eli Terry's residence in Terryville according to his obituary on February 21, 1852, which contradicts the fact that the Terrysville Post Office was established on December 22, 1831, and it was not until sometime after 1872 that the *s* was dropped and the town became Terryville. I'm certain that we, too, will not be errorless.

As relatively recent NAWCC members, we have appreciated meeting so many other members who have contributed to our growing clock knowledge and who have been so willing to share their stockpile of information and professional books with us. Being able to add their names to our growing list of friends has made this project a meaningful experience. For this and much more, Bob and Harriett say, "Thanks!"

2
Succinct Review of Horological History

Did You Know?

The National Association of Watch and Clock Collectors, Inc., or *NAWCC,* is a natinal organization for clock and watch collectors that sponsors educational meetings, shows, and seminars for its members. The assocation is located at 514 Poplar Street, Columbia, PA, 17512.

Timepiece and clock have different meanings. A timepiece indicates the time only and is abbreviated "T only." A clock, on the other hand, shows the time and also has some audible striking mechanism that gongs, rings, or chimes on the hour. Half and quarter hours may be sounded, too. Its abbreviation, "T & S," means "time and strike."

Between 1807 and 1810 clock maker Eli Terry used water-power-driven machines to produce identical interchangeable wooden parts to use in assembling mass-produced clocks. Because of this, he is credited with helping to introduce the factory system in the United States.

Ansonia, New Haven, Seth Thomas, Waterbury, E. Ingraham, Gilbert, and E. N. Welch were the seven firms that controlled the clock industry from 1850 into the twentieth century. Welch was taken over by Sessions in 1903, and Ansonia's machinery and some equipment was sold to the Soviet government and moved to the Soviet Union in 1929.

Manufacturers of brass sometimes produced clocks in order to sell more metal. Ansonia, for example, applied brass ornaments and decorations to many of its timepieces. The Waterbury Clock Company was an outgrowth of the brass industry, and the Bristol Brass and Clock Company was also active in its use of brass appendages. All of these firms were located in Connecticut. The use of mass-produced, inexpensive brass movements around 1840 helped to expand the metal market.

Inexpensive brass movements were made by the New Haven Clock Company, New

Haven, Connecticut, and sold to the Jerome Manufacturing Company. When Jerome declared bankruptcy in 1855, the company's assets were purchased by New Haven Clock Company. With its new case-making facilities, the company was able to produce complete (works and case) clocks.

Clock motive power changed over the years. Weights usually provided the power for clocks until about 1840 or 1850. After this, spring-driven movements generally prevailed. Electric clocks became popular in the 1930s.

A patent number enables you to date the piece on which it is found. For example, if a clock works bears the patent number 246,238, you can readily determine that this patent was issued in 1881 by referring to the Patent Date Chart in this chapter. Because patents are good for seventeen years, you can at least place 1881 as the earliest possible date on the clock works.

Labels should be preserved with care. They represent both a historical and a horological treasure. If a portion of the label is loose, carefully glue it to the backboard. Save even a portion of an existing label. It helps identify and date clocks. Collectors also treasure signed and dated movements and dials with company names on them.

A distributor's or jeweler's name sometimes appears on the dial of a clock.

Historical Events in Clockmaking

Sources often differ on dates, names, and other information relative to clocks. The use of "circa" (about) indicates an approximate time, give or take several years, before or after an indicated date. "Circa" may be abbreviated "c." or "ca." We have attempted to present facts as accurately as our research permits. In contrast to the hundreds of clockmakers in the United States, we mention only a small portion of that number here.

Chronology

Date	Event
Pre-1775 Colonial Period	Craftsmen made clocks to order, one at a time. This was an expensive process, and metal and glass were scarce. Brass movements were fashioned by hand with simple tools. Philadelphia was one center for the production of tall-case floor clocks, better known as grandfather clocks.
Circa 1760s	Benjamin Willard, the first of four clockmaking brothers, was at work at Grafton, Massachusetts, as was Simon, the most famous Willard. They made tall-case floor clocks. Brothers Ephraim and Aaron were making clocks a few years later. Aaron also became well known.
Circa 1760 to 1830	Simon and Aaron Willard made 30-hour wall timepieces. They and other clock men made the earliest known American shelf clock, called the Massachusetts half clock, which resembled the top of a tall-case floor clock.
1775 to 1783	During the American Revolution, clock production diminished as many clockmakers enlisted in or made war materiel for the Continental Army.

Date	Event
Circa 1790	Gideon Roberts, the first-known Bristol, Connecticut, clockmaker, made several clocks at a time and found a way to produce less expensive wooden movements to replace handmade brass works.

To this point, no examples of the museum-quality clocks mentioned in the chronology appear in this book. The list of craftsmen is long, and examples of their creative efforts as found in museums are rarely available to purchasers. Clocks were handcrafted in all of the thirteen colonies as well as in the frontier areas, including Kentucky, Maine, Ohio, and Vermont, the fourteeth state.

Date	Event
1793	Following the completion of his apprenticeship, Eli Terry began making clocks near Plymouth, Connecticut.
1802	Simon Willard patented his "Improved Timepiece," later called "banjo" because of its shape. Originally, most examples were time only. This clock style has been copied consistently over the years.
1807 to 1810	Eli Terry contracted to make an unheard-of 4,000 hang-up clock movements at four dollars each in three years' time. The water-power-driven machines he designed produced identical interchangeable wooden parts for inexpensive (grandfather type) clock works. Silas Hoadley and Seth Thomas worked for him. Terry is credited with introducing the factory system of mass production to the industry. This helped start the factory system in the United States, and inexpensive clocks, made in quantities, became available to the general public.
	Various craftsmen made wag on the wall clocks. They had dials, hands, and wooden works. Weights and the long pendulum were exposed to view, with the pendulum swinging back and forth (wagging on the wall). Actually these were tall-case floor-clock movements without the case. They cost less and were easier for peddlers to transport. Purchasers could make their own cases or have craftsmen make them, or they could hang the clocks on the wall as they were. Similar clocks were also made in colonial times, but with brass works.
Circa 1810 to 1813	Seth Thomas and Silas Hoadley bought Terry's Plymouth, Connecticut, clock shop. Thomas sold out in 1813 and Hoadley continued in business.
1811 to the late 1830s	Six Ives brothers, including Joseph and Chauncey, were involved in the clock industry.
1813	Seth Thomas set up his own shop in Plymouth Hollow, Connecticut, where he became a prolific clockmaker.
1816	Eli Terry patented a pillar-and-scroll shelf clock with a 30-hour wooden works that evolved from his plain box-type case.
	Chauncey Jerome made clock cases for Eli Terry for a short time.
Circa 1818	Joseph Ives made a brass clock movement with steel plates.
1820 to 1830	Circumventing Terry's patent, other companies varied the pillar-and-scroll clock, frequently using brass 8-day movements.

Date	Event
1822	Joseph Ives of Bristol, Connecticut, patented a looking-glass clock, but Aaron Willard, Jr., claimed that Massachusetts makers had been using looking glasses to add variety to clock fronts for some twenty-five years.
Circa 1825	Before 1825 Joseph Ives had learned how to make rolled brass. He moved to Brooklyn, New York, where he stayed briefly and invented the wagon spring to power a clock. The wagon spring is a series of flat-leaved arched springs that resemble those used in wagons.
	Chauncey Jerome patented a "bronze looking glass clock" with a 30-hour wooden movement, using a mirror instead of a tablet, and bronze-colored pilasters. Jerome specialized in case building and usually bought his movements from others. Also at this time Jerome, Darrow and Company, Bristol, Connecticut, became clockmakers.
Circa 1825 to 1920	OG, or ogee, the S-curved veneer-framed clocks, were made and sold widely throughout this ninety-five year period. They were prolonged best-sellers.
Circa 1827	Clockmaker Elias Ingraham was recorded at work.
Circa 1830	George Mitchell and Rollin and Irenus Atkins were making clocks in Bristol, Connecticut.
	Mark Leavenworth of Waterbury, Connecticut, made wooden movements for clocks.
	Marsh, Gilbert & Company operated a clock business in Bristol, Connecticut.
1830	Eli Terry's son, Silas B. Terry, patented a method for tempering coiled springs so they could be produced inexpensively.
After 1830	Rolled brass became more available for clock movements. Chauncey Jerome gave his brother Noble an idea for replacing wooden clock works with inexpensive rolled-brass movements. Some authorities feel that Chauncey copied Joseph Ives's mirror clock and his brass movement.
1831	Terrysville Post Office was established on December 22, 1831.
1831 to 1837	Burr & Chittenden were making clocks in Lexington, Massachusetts.
Circa 1831	J. C. Brown was making clocks in Bristol, Connecticut.
Circa 1832	Daniel Pratt, Jr., was a clockmaker in Reading, Massachusetts.
1836	James S. Ives of Bristol received a patent for brass-coiled clock springs.
1837 to 1843	The firm of Birge & Mallory was making clocks.
1839	Chauncey Jerome patented his rolled-brass movement to replace wooden movements.

Date	Event
Circa 1840s	Elias Ingraham, Bristol, Connecticut, designed a sharp Gothic clock popularly called "steeple."
Circa 1840s–50s	Weight-driven clocks were gradually replaced by spring-driven ones.
1842	Howard & Davis, Boston, was manufacturing clocks.
1842 to 1849	J. C. Brown became J. C. Brown & Company and also used the name Forestville Manufacturing Company.
1849	American Clock Company, New York City, was organized as a large depository to sell clocks made by various companies. The company issued catalogues of wares.
	Silas Hoadley retired after a successful clockmaking career.
Up to the 1850s	Hundreds of different stencils were used in the painting of clock tablets.
Circa 1850	Brass-coiled springs were largely replaced by better and cheaper steel springs.
	Nicholas Muller was at work as a founder in New York City. He made the iron front clock.
1850	Ansonia Clock Company was established in Ansonia, Connecticut, by Anson Phelps.
1851	Samuel Emerson Root was at work in Bristol, Connecticut, where he made some marine-type movements.
Circa 1851	Wm. L. Gilbert Clock Company, Winsted, Connecticut, began after various partnerships were terminated.
1853	Seth Thomas Clock Company, Plymouth, Connecticut, was incorporated.
	Hiram Camp started the New Haven Clock Company in New Haven, Connecticut.
	John H. Hawes of Ithaca, New York, patented the first-known simple-mechanism calendar clock.
After 1853	Many patents were issued for calendar clocks.
1854	A fire at the Ansonia Clock Company forced the company to move to Phelps's mill under the new name of Ansonia Brass and Copper Company.
1855	New Haven Clock Company took over Jerome Manufacturing Company and continued to use the Jerome name.
	John C. Briggs of Concord, New Hampshire, received a patent for a clock escapement called "Briggs Rotary."
1857	Waterbury Clock Company began operations in Waterbury, Connecticut.
	Elias Ingraham began The E. Ingraham Clock Company in Bristol, Connecticut.

Date	Event
1859	Seth Thomas died.
Circa 1859	La Porte Hubbell and Levi Beach were clockmakers in Bristol.
1859 to 1861	L. F. and W. W. Carter were partners in Bristol with Elias Burwell.
Circa 1863	F. Kroeber manufactured clocks in New York City, making fine cases and often altering purchased movements.
1863 to 1868	L. F. and W. W. Carter were making calendar clocks.
1864	Mozart, Beach & Hubbell patented a perpetual-calendar clock that needed to be wound only once a year.
	E. N. Welch, Bristol, Connecticut, consolidated the clock companies he purchased under the E. N. Welch Manufacturing Company name.
1865	The Ithaca Calendar Clock Company was established; it used Henry B. Horton's perpetual roller-type calendar clock patent.
1866	Plymouth Hollow became Thomaston, Connecticut, to honor the Thomas name. As a result, clock labels were changed to "Thomaston."
1867	The battery-operated electric clock was marketed.
	Alfonso Broadman, Forestville, Connecticut, made a simple calendar clock with two rollers, one for the month and the date and the other for the day of the week.
1868	A partnershsip was formed and named the Welch, Spring & Company. The company made regulator and calendar clocks.
	Joseph K. Seem's patent showed the way to attach three small disks to the back of an existing clock dial, making it a simple calendar clock.
1868 to 1893	Parker & Whipple Company operated in Meriden, Connecticut.
1869	Celluloid, a flammable plastic, was developed. It was later used on clock cases to simulate tortoiseshell, amber, onyx, and other materials.
1870s to 1880s	George Owen, Winsted, Connecticut, had a small shop that later merged with Gilbert Company.
1871	Daniel Gale, Sheboygan, Wisconsin, patented an astronomical calendar clock dial.
1872	Terrysville, Connecticut, became Terryville.
	Joseph K. Seem obtained a patent for a perpetual-calendar roller mechanism that could be fitted on top of an existing clock when space permitted. He moved to Macomb, Illinois from Canton, Pennsylvania.
1879	Ansonia Clock Company moved to Brooklyn, New York. Clocks marked "New York" appeared.

Date	Event
Circa 1880	Nicholas Muller's Sons made fancy shelf-clock cases of iron and bronze.
1880	H. J. Davis made an illuminated alarm clock.
1881	Joseph K. Seem was granted a patent that improved his 1872 perpetual calendar mechanism.
1881 to 1885	Yale Clock Company, New Haven, Connecticut, advertised novelty clocks.
1882	The Macomb Calendar Clock Company was formed in Illinois. The company used Seem's 1881 calendar clock patent.
1883	The Macomb Calendar Clock Company went out of business.
	A. C. Clausen patented the "Ignatz" (flying pendulum) clock.
	Benjamin Franklin, Chicago, patented a perpetual calendar clock mechanism that could be attached to an existing clock by cutting a hole in its dial.
1885	The Sidney Advertising Clock, Sidney, New York, developed a large wall clock on which advertising drums turned every five minutes.
1886 to 1916	Darche Electric Clock Company, Chicago and Jersey City, New Jersey, made battery-alarm timepieces.
Circa 1888	The Loheide Manufacturing Company, St. Louis, Missouri, was established.
	The Self Winding Clock Company, New York City and Brooklyn, made battery-powered and electric clocks.
1890	Edward P. Baird & Company was established in Plattsburgh, New York. It used Seth Thomas works. The company's papier-mâché advertising clocks were a specialty.
Circa 1890	Jennings Brothers Manufacturing Company of Bridgeport, Connecticut, were making metal clocks.
1891 to 1897	Henry Prentiss of New York City received various patents for calendar mechanisms that ran for one year after being wound.
1893	Parker & Whipple Company became Parker Clock Company.
1895	Western Clock Manufacturing Company began in La Salle, Illinois.
1896 to 1900	Edward P. Baird & Company moved to Evanston, Illinois, where they made wooden-case clocks with metal dials rimmed with embossed and painted advertisements.
1897	Chelsea Clock Company was operating in Chelsea, Massachusetts. The company's output included auto and ship clocks as well as those for homes.
Late 1800s	Simplex Company of Gardner, Massachusetts, was making time recorders and time clocks.
	Decalcomania transfers were common on clock tablets.

Date	Event
1902	John Peatfield of Arlington, Massachusetts, patented a perpetual calendar with a spring-driven mechanism that was wound yearly.
1903	Sessions Clock Company, Bristol-Forestville, Connecticut, bought E. N. Welch Manufacturing Company.
1908	The Loheide Manufacturing Company of St. Louis, Missouri, patented a slot-machine clock.
1910	"Big Ben" alarm clocks were being made.
1915	"Little Ben" alarm clocks were being made.
Circa 1917	Paul Lux of Waterbury, Connecticut, founded the Lux Clock Manufacturing Company and produced many novelty clocks. He used molded wood cases. He also made clocks under the name De Luxe.
1929	International Business Machine Corporation, Endicott, New York, was organized.
	Ansonia Clock Company equipment and materials were purchased by and moved to the Soviet Union.
1931	August C. Keebler of Chicago founded the August C. Keebler Company, which marketed Lux Clocks, including the pendulettes that he sold to large mail-order companies. He did not make clocks, but his name was sometimes used on Lux Clocks.
1936	Westclox, a trade name, became the new name for Western Clock Manufacturing Company.
	Hammond Clock Company of Chicago was in operation.

Leading Clock Manufacturers

Eli Terry

Date	Historical Development
1792 to 1793	Eli Terry, Sr., was at work making tall-case clocks. Both brass and wooden works were made near East Windsor, Connecticut, and then near what became the Thomaston and Plymouth area.
1800	One of the few clockmakers making several wooden-movement clocks at a time. He used saws driven by water power.
1806 to 1809	Fulfilled a contract to make 4,000 hang-up wooden clock movements, pendulums, dials, and hands. Invented machines to aid work, including one to cut gear-wheel teeth. Employed Seth Thomas and Silas Hoadley to assist him. Worked near Waterbury, where more water power was available.
1810	Sold plant to Thomas and Hoadley and moved to Plymouth Hollow, Connecticut.
Circa 1816	Patented a shelf clock with a new outside escapement movement in a pillar-and-scroll case.
Circa 1818 to 1824	Became Eli Terry & Sons, Plymouth, Connecticut. Eli Sr., Eli Jr., and Henry produced many pillar and scroll clocks. The label stated, "Patent clock invented by Eli Terry made and sold at Plymouth, Connecticut by Eli Terry and Sons. . ." The 8-day triple-decker clock was made 34 to 38 inches high to accommodate the longer fall of the weights. The 30-hour clock case required less height.
1824 to 1827	Eli and Samuel Terry at work in Plymouth. Eli and brother Samuel listed together on clock labels.
1824 to 1830	Eli Terry, Jr., label used in Plymouth.
1825 to 1830	Eli Terry and son Henry in clock business in Plymouth.
1830 to 1841	Eli Terry, Jr. & Company located in Plymouth, which soon became Terrysville.
1831 to 1837	Henry Terry, in Terrysville, continued the business he and his father had in Plymouth.
1831	The Terrysville Post Office was established.
Circa 1834	Eli Terry, Sr., retired after a financially successful career. He made some brass-movement clocks after his retirement.
Late 1840s	S. B. Terry & Company located in Terrysville. Silas Burnham was Eli Sr.'s youngest son.
1852	Eli Terry, Sr., died in Terrysville.
1852	The Terry Clock Company was organized by Silas Burnham Terry and his sons in Winsted, Connecticut, with Silas as its president.
1852 to 1876	The Terry Clock Company was in business.
After 1872	By dropping the s, the Terrysville Post office name was changed to Terryville, Connecticut.

Seth Thomas

Date	Historical Development
Early 1800s	Seth Thomas apprenticed in the cabinetmaker-joiner trade.
Circa 1808 to 1810	Seth Thomas, carpenter, and Silas Hoadley worked under Eli Terry near Waterbury, Connecticut, to help Terry fulfill his contract for 4,000 hang-up wooden clock movements, pendulums, dials, and hands. Thomas was the joiner and also assembled the clocks—fitting the wheels and different parts in their proper places and putting clocks in running condition.
1810	Seth Thomas and Silas Hoadley bought Eli Terry's plant. The partners made 30-hour wooden-movement clocks and tall-case clocks.
1813	Seth Thomas sold out to Silas Hoadley and bought a shop in Plymouth Hollow, Connecticut. He made tall-case clocks with wooden movements.
1813 to 1853	Seth Thomas in operation in Plymouth Hollow, Connecticut.
Circa 1816	Said to have paid Eli Terry for the right to make wooden-movement shelf clocks. The label read, "Patent Clocks Eli Terry, Inventor and Patentee Made & Sold by Seth Thomas, Plymouth, Conn."
1839	Changed production from wooden to 30-hour brass movements.
Circa 1850	Began to use springs instead of weights as clock power.
1853 to 1865	Seth Thomas Clock Company in operation in Plymouth Hollow, Connecticut.
1859	Seth Thomas died and sons Aaron, Edward, and Seth Jr. carried on business.
1866	Plymouth Hollow became Thomaston in honor of the Thomas clock family.
	Seth Thomas' Sons & Company was formed to make marine escapement movements. The company also made fine pendulum 18-day spring-driven movements.
1879	Seth Thomas Sons & Company was consolidated with the Seth Thomas Clock Company.
1931	The Seth Thomas Clock Company, established in 1853, became a division of General Time Instrument Company.
1932	Seth Thomas's great grandson, Seth E. Thomas, Jr., was chairman of the board until his death in 1932, at which time the company's leadership passed out of the hands of the Thomas family.
1949	The Seth Thomas Clock Company became a division of General Time Corporation.
1970	The Seth Thomas Clock Company became a division of Tally Industries and remains in operation today.

Waterbury Clock Company

Date	Historical Development
1850	Benedict & Burnham Manufacturing Company made brass products and went into the clock business. The company went through various name changes.
1857	The Waterbury Clock Company, Waterbury, Connecticut, was formed as a branch of Benedict & Burnham. The company made all kinds of shelf clocks and some tall-case clocks.
1892	Made watches for Ingersoll. Waterbury sold movements it made in addition to total clocks, including round-top and octagon-drop regulators, calendar clocks, and many versions for the home.
1922	Purchased the Robert H. Ingersoll & Brother watch business.
1944	Became a part of U.S. Time Corporation.

Ansonia Clock Company

Ansonia Brass Company, Ansonia, Connecticut, was started by Anson Phelps, an importer of tin, copper, and brass. He built a rolling mill for sheet brass.

Date	Historical Development
1850	Anson Phelps started the Ansonia Clock Company near Derby, Connecticut. This helped increase the sale of brass for both movements and decorative touches.
1851 to 1878	Ansonia Brass and Clock Company was also called the Ansonia Clock Company.
1854	Fire destroyed the factory. The company relocated at Phelps's mill and produced clocks under the name of The Ansonia Brass and Copper Company.
1878	The Ansonia Clock Company was reformed to manufacture clocks.
1879	Moved to Brooklyn, New York. Soon fire destroyed the plant.
1880	The Ansonia Clock Company was reactivated in Brooklyn. All types of shelf and wall clocks were made, many with brass embellishments. Novelties, such as the "Bobbing Doll" and "Swinging Doll" were made, as well as imitation French clocks. The clocks were marked "New York."
1929	Machines and some equipment were sold to the Soviet government and moved to the Soviet Union.

New Haven Clock Company

Date	Historical Development
1853	The New Haven Clock Company was organized with Hiram Camp (Chauncey Jerome's nephew) as president. The company made inexpensive brass movements for the Jerome Manufacturing Company.
1855	Purchased the bankrupt Jerome Manufacturing Company.
1856	With the Jerome Manufacturing Company's facilities in New Haven, the company now made cases as well as movements to create whole clocks.
Circa 1880	New Haven had sales offices in Chicago, England, and Japan. It sold its own and Kroeber, Ingraham, and E. Howard clocks. Became one of the largest clock companies in the United States.
1885	Marketed only New Haven clocks, except for a few imported brands.
1910	Offered a vast variety of clocks—almost too diversified to do well.
1917 to 1956	Became a major producer of inexpensive watches.
1946	A corporation called New Haven Clock and Watch Company took over the company.
1956 to 1959	The company faced financial difficulties.
1960	The company's manufacturing facilities were sold at auction.

E. N. Welch Manufacturing Company

Date	Historical Development
Before 1831	Elisha Niles Welch was in foundry business with father, George, making clock bells and weights.
1831 to 1834	Thomas Barnes and Welch manufactured wooden-movement shelf clocks under the name Barnes & Welch.
1841 to 1849	J. C. Brown used both Forestville Manufacturing Company and J. C. Brown, Bristol, Connecticut, as company names. E. N. Welch became a partner with him and Chauncey Pomeroy in 1841 in the Forestville Manufacturing Company in Bristol. The company made 8-day brass-movement clocks.
1853	Fire destroyed Brown's Forestville company.
Circa 1854	Elisha Manross was making clock parts. When he failed, E. Welch bought his firm.
1856	Purchased the bankrupt J. C. Brown Forestville Company.
	F. N. Otis of Bristol made shelf clocks with fancy pearl-inlay cases. The company failed and E. N. Welch acquired his business.
1864	Became one of the largest Bristol clock companies when Welch consolidated all his companies under the E. N. Welch name. Made quality clocks.

Date	Historical Development
1868 to 1884	Partnership formed to become Welch, Spring and Company, Bristol. Made quality regulator and calendar clocks. Spring sold his previously purchased Birge, Peck and Company to the new firm, and Welch gave the Manross factory to it. The company made high-quality clocks but was not successful and was absorbed by E. N. Welch in 1884.
1887	Elisha Niles Welch died and his son James became president of E. N. Welch. Financial problems followed.
1899	The E. N. Welch movement factory was destroyed by fire, and at the end of the year the case factory burned.
1902	James Welch died. The company's financial problems increased. The Session family bought stock.
1903	W. E. Sessions and A. L. Sessions invested money in the company and changed the name to the Sessions Clock Company.

William L. Gilbert Clock Company

Date	Historical Development
1828	George Marsh and William L. Gilbert bought a clock shop and formed Marsh, Gilbert & Company.
1828 to 1834	Marsh, Gilbert & Company was active in Bristol and Farmington, Connecticut.
1835 to 1837	Formed Birge, Gilbert & Company in Bristol with John Birge and manufactured Empire-style shelf clocks.
1839 to 1840	Jerome, Grant, Gilbert & Company was formed with Chauncey and Noble Jerome and Zelotas Grant to produce Jerome's inexpensive brass-movement clocks.
1841	Gilbert and Lucius Clarke bought a clock factory in Winchester (Winsted), Connecticut. Ezra Baldwin joined the business.
1814 to 1845	Clarke, Gilbert & Company produced inexpensive brass clocks.
1845 to 1848	W. L. Gilbert & Company formed when Gilbert bought Clarke's share in the company.
1848	Clarke bought back his share and Gilbert & Clarke was formed.
1848 to 1851	Gilbert & Clarke operated a clock business.
1851 to 1866	Firm name changed to W. L. Gilbert & Company in 1851 and continued as such until 1866.
1866 to 1871	The Gilbert Manufacturing Company was in business.
1871	The Winsted factory burned down.
1871 to 1934	The William L. Gilbert Clock Company was formed in 1871 and remained active for these sixty-one years in Winsted, Connecticut.
1880 to circa 1900	Under George B. Owen's management, the company expanded.

Date	Historical Development
1890	William Lewis Gilbert died.
Circa 1934 to 1957	Various years brought financial reverses, but the company continued and became William L. Gilbert Clock Corporation.
1941 to 1945	The U.S. government permitted the company to manufacture papier-mâché clocks, especially alarm clocks, since metal was needed for World War II and alarm clocks were in demand.
1957 to 1964	General Computing Machines Company took over the company, which operated under the name General-Gilbert Corporation.
1964	The unprofitable clock division was purchased by Spartus Corporation of Louisville, Mississippi, and Chicago.

The E. Ingraham Company

Date	Historical Development
1828 to 1830	After a five-year apprenticeship as a cabinetmaker and joiner, Elias Ingraham designed clock cases for George Mitchell of Bristol, Connecticut, including one with carved mahogany columns, paw feet, carved baskets of fruit, and turned rosettes. He became the foremost clock-case designer of his era.
1830 to 1833	Designed cases for Chauncey and Lawson C. Ives, including an Empire-style triple-decker clock.
1831 to 1832	Under the name of Ingraham & Bartholomew, Ingraham and William G. Bartholomew of Bristol, Connecticut, built a cabinet-making shop to produce clock cases. In 1832 Ingraham sold out to J. C. Brown.
1832 to 1833	Under the company name of Ingraham & Goodrich, Ingraham and Chauncey Goodrich made cases in Bristol.
1835 to 1840	Bought a shop in Bristol and manufactured clock cases, chairs, and mirrors. Had financial problems for a time.
Circa 1840	Designed the sharp Gothic case called the "steeple" clock. One of the most popular shelf-clock styles ever, it is still being made today.
1841 to 1844	Ray and Ingraham at work in Bristol.
1844 to 1852	Brewster & Ingrahams formed. Elias and brother Andrew in partnership with Elisha C. Brewster.
Circa 1852 to 1855	Elias at work with his brother Andrew in Bristol under the name of E. & A. Ingraham.
	Ingrahams & Stedman was formed when Andrew Ingraham sold half of his interest in the firm to Edward C. Stedman.
1855	The Ingraham factory burned down.

Date	Historical Development
1855 to 1856	The Ingrahams were located in Ansonia, Connecticut, and sold clocks with the E. & A. Ingraham and Company label.
1856	The Ingrahams bought out Stedman and the partnership was dissolved.
1857 to 1861	Elias Ingraham & Company was in operation.
1861 to 1880	The name E. Ingraham & Company was used.
1881 to 1884	The E. Ingraham & Company, Bristol, was in operation.
1884	The company was incorporated as The E. Ingraham Company, Bristol.
1885	Elias Ingraham died.
	Clocks with japanned or black-painted cases were successfully marketed in more than 200 different case styles.
1914	Nonjeweled pocket watches were sold.
After 1915	Lever-movement 8-day clocks were being produced.
1930	Wristwatches were marketed.
After 1931	Electric clocks were being made.
1941 to 1959	The company expanded, establishing plants in Toronto, Canada; Elizabethtown, Kentucky; and Laurinburg, North Carolina.
1967	The company was sold to McGraw-Edison, a conglomerate. Clockmaking ceased in Bristol.
	Electric and battery-powered clocks were made in Laurinburg, North Carolina.
	The name Ingraham became a trademark.

Patent Numbers and Dates Issued

Year	Patent No.	Year	Patent No.	Year	Patent No.
1836	1	1880	223,211	1924	1,478,996
1837	110	1881	236,137	1925	1,521,590
1838	516	1882	251,685	1926	1,568,040
1839	1,061	1883	269,820	1927	1,612,790
1840	1,465	1884	291,016	1928	1,654,521
		1885	310,163	1929	1,696,897
1841	1,923	1886	333,494		
1842	2,413	1887	355,291	1930	1,742,181
1843	2,901	1888	375,720	1931	1,787,424
1844	3,395	1889	395,305	1932	1,839,190
1845	3,873			1933	1,892,663
1846	4,348	1890	418,665	1934	1,944,449
1847	4,914	1891	443,987	1935	1,985,878
1848	5,409	1892	466,315	1936	2,026,510
1849	5,993	1893	488,976	1937	2,066,309
		1894	511,744	1938	2,101,004
1850	6,981	1895	531,619	1939	2,142,080
1851	7,865	1896	552,502		
1852	8,622	1897	574,369	1940	2,185,170
1853	9,512	1898	596,467	1941	2,227,418
1854	10,358	1899	616,871	1942	2,268,540
1855	12,117			1943	2,307,007
1856	14,009	1900	640,167	1944	2,338,081
1857	16,324	1901	664,827	1945	2,366,154
1858	19,010	1902	690,385	1946	2,391,856
1859	22,477	1903	717,521	1947	2,413,675
1860	26,642	1904	748,567	1948	2,433,824
1861	31,005	1905	778,834	1949	2,457,797
1862	34,045	1906	808,618		
1863	37,266	1907	839,799	1950	2,492,944
1864	41,047	1908	875,679	1951	2,536,016
1865	45,685	1909	908,436	1952	2,580,379
1866	51,784			1953	2,624,018
1867	60,658	1910	945,010	1954	2,664,562
1868	72,959	1911	980,178	1955	2,698,431
1869	85,503	1912	1,013,095	1956	2,728,913
		1913	1,049,326	1957	2,775,762
1870	98,460	1914	1,083,267	1958	2,818,567
1871	110,617	1915	1,123,212	1959	2,866,973
1872	122,304	1916	1,166,419		
1873	134,504	1917	1,210,389	1960	2,919,443
1874	146,120	1918	1,251,458	1961	2,966,681
1875	158,350	1919	1,290,027	1962	3,015,103
1876	171,641			1963	3,070,801
1877	185,813	1920	1,326,899	1964	3,116,487
1878	198,733	1921	1,364,063		
1879	211,078	1922	1,401,948		
		1923	1,440,362		

Calendar Clock Inventors

Inventor	Residence	Patent Date
Randal T. Andrews	Thomaston, Conn.	Feb. 15, 1876
William H. Atkins and Joseph C. Burritt	Ithaca, N. Y.	Sept. 19, 1854 Nov. 17, 1857
Alfonzo Boardman	Forestville, Conn.	July 2, 1867
Charles M. Clinton and Lynfred Mood	Ithaca, N. Y.	June 25, 1867 Nov. 11, 1867
Alfred A. Cowles	New York, N. Y.	July 13, 1875
Charles W. Feishtinger	Fritztown, Pa.	Oct. 9, 1894
Benjamin Franklin	Chicago, Ill.	June 12, 1883
Daniel J. Gale	Sheboygan, Wis.	June 19, 1877 April 21, 1885
John H. H. Hawes	Ithaca, N. Y.	May 17, 1853
Henry B. Horton	Ithaca, N. Y.	April 18, 1865 Aug. 28, 1866
F. Kroeber	Hoboken, N. J.	July 31, 1877
Benjamin B. Lewis	Bristol, Conn.	Feb. 4, 1862 June 21, 1864 Dec. 29, 1868 Nov. 15, 1881
T. W. R. McCabe	Winston, Conn.	Nov. 10, 1896
Galusha Maranville	Winston, Conn.	Mar. 5, 1861
James E. and Eugene M. Mix	Bristol, Conn.	Jan. 31, 1860 April 4, 1862
Don J. Mozart, Levi Beach, and LaPorte Hubbel	New York, N. Y., Farmington, Conn., Bristol, Conn.	Jan. 5, 1864
George B. Owen	New York, N. Y.	April 24, 1866
John I. Peatfield	Arlington, Mass.	July 15, 1902
Albert Phelps	Ansonia, Conn.	Dec. 5, 1876
Henry S. Prentiss	New York, N. Y.	April 14, 1891
Josiah K. Seem	Canton, Pa., Macomb, Ill.	Jan. 7, 1868 Dec. 24, 1872 Dec. 13, 1881
William A. Terry	Bristol, Conn.	June 16, 1868 Jan. 25, 1870 July 13, 1875
A. F. Wells	Friendship, N. Y.	July 30, 1889
James E. Young	Genoa, N. Y.	June 19, 1883

Ansonia "Antique" oak floor clock (grandfather clock) with brass trim; 8-day, time and strike, weight driven, pictured in 1886 and 1914 catalogues; $20\frac{1}{2}''$ wide, 94'' high, $9\frac{1}{2}''$ dial; **$5,000.**

Ansonia ''Utopia'' brass-plated crystal regulator with open escapement; 8-day, time and strike, spring driven; 8¾" deep, 18" high; **$2,500**; *Ansonia ''Jupiter'' brass-plated crystal regulator with open escapement and porcelain dial; 8-day, time and strike, spring driven; 8¾" deep, 18" high;* **$2,250**. *Both clocks were pictured in 1914 catalogue.*

Ansonia ''Melody and the Dancer'' brass-washed metal shelf clock with open escapement and porcelain dial; 8-day, time and strike, spring driven; 24" wide, 22" high; **$1,500.**

American Clock Company metal case shelf clock; 30-hour, time and strike, spring driven; 13" wide, 16" high, 3½" dial; **$275.** *Jerome and Company fuzee shelf clock with papier mâché case and mother-of-pearl inlay; 8-day, time and strike, spring driven; 10½" wide, 14" high, 5" dial;* **$500.**

Ansonia "Cabinet E" oak shelf clock with brass trim; 8-day, time and strike, spring driven; 12" wide, 18¼" high, 5" dial; **$350.** *Nicholas Muller cast-iron shelf clock with warrior statue; 8-day, time and strike, spring driven; 16" wide, 18¼" high, 4½" dial;* **$500.**

Ansonia ''Lydia'' brass-plated metal shelf clock; 8-day, time and strike, spring driven with porcelain shield numbers on brass dial, circa 1900; 12" wide, 21" high; **$1,500.**

Ansonia ''Antique'' oak wall clock with brass trim; 8-day, time and strike, weight driven, pictured in 1886 and 1914 catalogues; 16½" wide, 45" high; **$4,800.**

Ansonia ''Fortuna'' brass-plated, swinging arm, metal shelf clock; 8-day, time only, spring driven; 10" wide, 29½" high; **$2,500.**

Ansonia Royal Bonn porcelain shelf clock; 8-day, time and strike, spring driven, early 1900s; 8" wide, 17" high; **$800.** *Ansonia crystal shelf clock with Royal Bonn porcelain base and top, early 1900s; 8-day, time and strike, spring driven; 8" wide, 17" high;* **$2,250.**

Ansonia "Cabinet Antique" walnut shelf clock with brass trim and porcelain dial; 8-day, time and bell strike on top, 11½" wide, 18" high; **$1,200.** *Ansonia "Cabinet D" oak shelf clock with brass trim; 8-day, strike and time, spring driven; 11½" wide, 24" high;* **$800.**

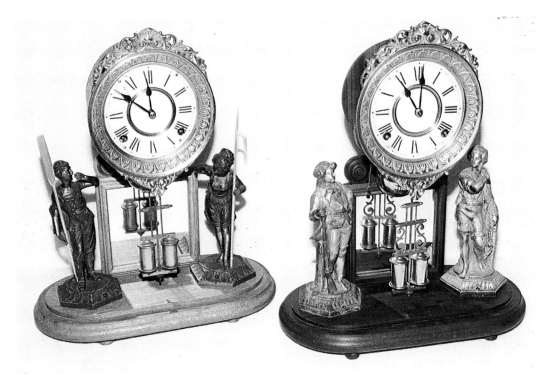

Ansonia "Crystal Palace" oak-based, cylinder pendulum shelf clock with oarsman and helmsman statues; 14" wide, 17" high, 5" dial; **$500.** *Ansonia "Crystal Palace" walnut-based, cylinder pendulum shelf clock with hunter and fisherman statues; 14" wide, 17" high, 5" dial;* **$500.** *Glass domes, not pictured, are available for both clocks.*

W. L. Gilbert "Amphion" walnut shelf clock with etched designs on mirrored panels and tablet; 8-day, time and strike, spring driven; 17" wide, 25" high, 5" dial; **$750.**

Ansonia "Queen Elizabeth" oak wall clock, awarded a prize medal at the Paris Exposition in 1878 as indicated by the label on the back of the case; 8-day, time and strike; 13½" wide, 38" high, 7¼" dial; **$800.**

Ansonia iron shelf clock with brass knight and digital reading on velvet background; time only, tandem spring driven; 7" wide, 21" high; **$800.**

Lux "Harvest Time" composition case shelf clock 1920s–1940s; 8-day, time only, spring driven; 11" wide, 17" high; **$250.**

Ansonia ebony-finished wall clock with gilt designs and mirrors at the sides and a Mary Gregory-type etched design on tablet, circa 1880; 8-day, time and strike, spring driven; 14" wide, 35" high; **$800.**

L. Hubbell Clock Company Reed's Tonic cherry shelf clock, dated 1865; 8-day, time only, spring driven; 10½" wide, 24" high; **$700.**

Ansonia shelf clock with majolica elephant base; 30-hour, time only, spring driven; 11" long, 10" high; $750.

Ansonia Royal Bonn porcelain shelf clock with open escapement and porcelain dial; 8-day, time only, spring driven; 14" wide, 14" high; $600.

Westclox Big Ben alarm clock on store display case; 30-hour, time, alarm and spring driven, patented February 10, 1914; no price available. New Haven "The Automatic" alarm clock on store display stand; 8-day, time and alarm, spring driven, patented October 20, 1908; no price available.

3
Old Timers

Did You Know?

It was a status symbol in the 1700s to own a clock. Clocks were handcrafted, one at a time, and were made only when an affluent person placed an order for one. The clockmaker frequently melted down the brass in his own furnace, cast it, hammered it, turned it, and filed it. The dial, the hands, the works, the case—the total clock—were completed in the shop. Apprentices assisted as they learned the trade. Very few people could afford to buy a clock so painstakingly constructed.

During the 1770s brass founders did the initial preparation of the metal. By 1780, however, cast-brass parts could be purchased, and the clockmaker did the turning, gear cutting, filing, and assembly. The industry was beginning to diversify as different craftsmen became involved in the clockmaking process.

Wooden movements that were easier to make and less costly than hand-fashioned brass movements came into use around 1800.

Paper dials in books of 24, 48, or 96 could be purchased in the late 1700s. These were pasted on wooden panels or iron plates to form clock faces.

Clock works run by falling weights required large cases to provide an adequate dropping space. For this reason, early weight-driven shelf clocks were tall.

Clocks with heavy weights were expensive to ship. Because of this, empty "tin cans" (sheet-iron cans), instead of the heavy weights, were shipped with the clocks. The recipient then could fill these containers with sand or stones to achieve the weight necessary to operate the clock properly.

When clocks were no longer made one at a time to fill individual orders, clockmakers often became itinerant merchants to sell their surplus supplies. Peddlers were also employed. In general, clock cases were not included because this reduced the cost to consumers, as well as the weight the peddlers had to carry. Since all the essential parts were there, customers could either hang up the clocks as they were or have cases made.

The banjo wall clock was patented by Simon Willard in 1802. He called it his "Improved Timepiece," but it was dubbed "banjo" because it resembled that instrument in shape. Originally they were time only.

The gilted girandole with a round base, designed by Lemuel Curtis between 1815 and 1818, was a variation of Simon Willard's banjo clock. It is considered to be one of America's most beautiful clocks.

The pillar-and-scroll clock was patented by Eli Terry in 1816. It evolved from his plain box case and had a 30-hour wooden works. Other makers varied the case somewhat so they could copy the idea without infringing on Terry's patent.

The looking-glass clock had a mirror tablet instead of the usual picture or design. Thrifty housewives liked the combination clock-mirror. Chauncey Jerome claimed it as his idea even though his "bronze looking glass clock" with its bronze-colored pilasters, which gave it its name, was patented about three years after Joseph Ives patented a looking-glass clock in 1822.

A scarce Mark Leavenworth pillar-and-scroll clock and its accompanying, uncommon Mark Leavenworth, Waterbury, Connecticut, label are pictured in this chapter. An 1820 census report is included inside the column where the left weight drops. Some of the facts listed record that New York, the largest state, had a population of 1,352,812 that year. Illinois, which had achieved statehood only two years before, had 55,211 residents. The 1825 postal rates are listed on the right side where the weight drops. Mark Leavenworth was well established in his own business prior to 1814 and sold wooden, uncased movements to other clockmakers.

Shelf clocks with wooden works usually contain 30-hour movements; 8-day examples are unusual.

Transition was the name given to certain clocks of the late 1820s, most of which had 30-hour weight-driven movements. They were carved or stenciled and had feet, frequently of the paw type. Often there were side columns, and a stenciled or carved top slat might be included. They were an in-between style, appearing about the time the pillar-and-scroll was high in popularity and the OG was new.

The OG (ogee) clock was a continuous favorite from around 1825 until 1920. Its box frame featured an OG (S-curved) veneered (usually mahogany) door molding and front. It had a decorated tablet. Early one-day weight-driven examples were approximately 26 inches high to accommodate the falling weights, whereas the 8-day type usually measured about 34 inches high. Later,

30-hour, 15-or-16-inch-high, spring-driven miniatures became available.

The following shows the exact words found on the backboard label of a Seth Thomas time-and-strike shelf clock with an alarm. The clock was made after the town name, Plymouth Hollow, was changed to Thomaston in 1866.

Thirty Hour Spring Clocks
Seth Thomas
Thomaston, Conn.
Warranted Good

Directions for setting the clock running. Place the clock in a perpendicular position. Oil the palletes or ends of the part commonly called the VERGE; the pin on which the Verge plays, and the wire which carries the pendulum, at the place where it touches the rod. One drop is sufficient for the whole. Hang on the pendulum ball, then put on key with handle down, and turn toward the figure VI and turn steadily until the clock is wound.

If the Clock should go too fast, lower the ball by means of a screw at the bottom of the pendulum; if too slow raise it.

If the hands want moving, do it by means of the longest, turning it at any time forward, but never backward, when the Clock is within fifteen minutes of striking; and in no case further than to carry the minute hand to the figure XII.

Should the Clock by any means strike wrong, it may be made to strike right by raising the small wire hanging near the bell.

Banjo Clocks

E. Howard & Company rosewood rounded-end box banjo wall clock, circa 1840; 8-day, time only; 11" wide at base, 28½" high, 7" dial; **$1,650.**

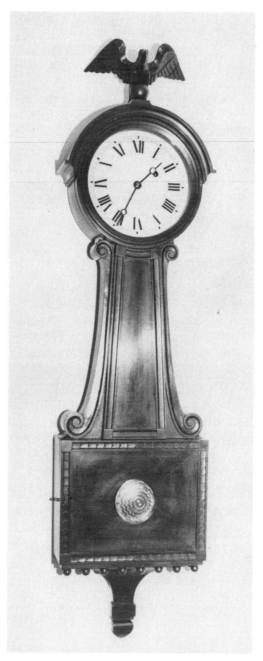

New Haven "Whitney" banjo wall clock with sidearms and eagle crown; 8-day, time and strike; 10" wide at base, 32" high; **$420.**

E. Howard & Company mahogany banjo wall clock with hand-carved wooden ball and eagle at crest, circa 1880; 8-day, time only, weight driven; 10" wide at base, 39" high, 7" dial; **$1,800.**

Sessions banjo wall clock with brass eagle and sidearms, circa 1880; 8-day, time only; 12½" wide at base, 42" high; $425.

Waterbury mahogany banjo wall clock with porcelain face, brass sidearms, circa 1908; 8-day, time only, weight driven; 10" wide at base, 42" high; $1,000.

Ansonia "Girandole" mahogany banjo wall clock with Westminster chimes, brass sidearms, and cut glass on throat and on round beveled glass door at base; 8-day, time and strike, spring driven; 12" diameter at base, 39" high, 8" dial; **$2,500.**

E. Ingraham "Nyanza" walnut-stained banjo wall clock, circa 1917; 8-day, time and strike; 10" wide at base, 38" high; **$325.**

Pillar-and-Scroll Clocks

E. Terry & Sons rosewood pillar-and-scroll shelf clock, wooden works, circa 1818–24; 30-hour, time and strike, weight driven; 17½" wide, 31" high; **$1,200.**

Mark Leavenworth mahogany-veneered and stained hardwoods pillar-and-scroll shelf clock, replaced brass finials, ivory escutcheon, circa 1825; 30-hour, time and strike, weight driven; 16¾" wide, 31" high; no price available.

Label from E. Terry & Sons pillar-and-scroll shelf clock.

Label from Mark Leavenworth pillar-and-scroll shelf clock.

Looking-Glass Clocks

Unknown maker, mahogany-veneered mirror (replaced) shelf clock, wooden works; 30-hour, time and strike, weight driven; 16½" wide, 35½" high; **$200.**

Eli Terry rosewood, mirror shelf clock with carved columns and eagle splat, wooden works, circa 1827; 30-hour, time and strike, weight driven; 20" wide, 37" high; **$975.**

Samuel Terry, Bristol, Connecticut, mahogany-veneered mirror shelf clock, with artificially grained columns and ivory escutcheon, circa 1829; 30-hour, time and strike, weight driven; 17" wide, 34" high; **$400.**

Mitchell, Atkins & Company, Bristol, Connecticut, mahogany-veneered mirror shelf clock with artificially grained columns and gold stenciling above dial, circa 1830–36; 30-hour, time, strike, and alarm, weight driven; 16½" wide, 32" high; no price available.

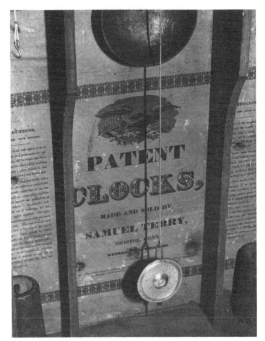

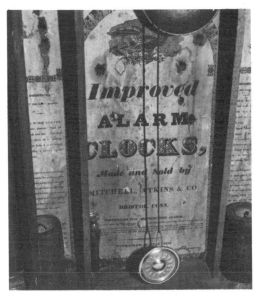

Label from Samuel Terry mirror shelf clock.

Label from Mitchell, Atkins & Company mirror shelf clock.

Label from Austin Chittenden mirror shelf clock.

Austin Chittenden rosewood, mirror shelf clock, wooden works, circa 1831–37; 30-hour, time, strike, and alarm, weight driven; 16" wide, 41" high; **$800.**

Transition Clocks

Eli Terry & Son mahogany shelf clock, wooden works, 1825–36; 30-hour, time and strike, weight driven; 17½" wide, 31" high; no price available.

*Ives-style Empire mahogany shelf clock, early 1800s; 8-day, time and strike, weight driven, brass strap movement; 18" wide, 35½" high, **$400.***

Label from Eli Terry & Son mahogany shelf clock.

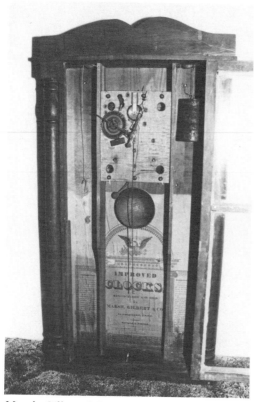

Marsh, Gilbert & Company mahogany-veneered shelf clock, wooden works, circa 1830; 30-hour, time and strike, weight driven; 17½" wide, 32½" high; **$375.**

Label from Marsh, Gilbert & Company mahogany-veneered shelf clock.

Closeup of mechanism showing wooden works in Marsh, Gilbert & Company mahogany-veneered shelf clock.

Eli Terry, Jr., mahogany-veneered shelf clock, wooden works, circa 1834–37; 30-hour, time and strike, weight driven; 16¾" wide, 26" high; **$800.**

Jerome, Darrow & Company rosewood shelf clock, wooden works, with President Jackson's Hermitage on tablet, circa 1825; 8-day, time and strike, weight driven; 19" wide, 40" high; **$800.**

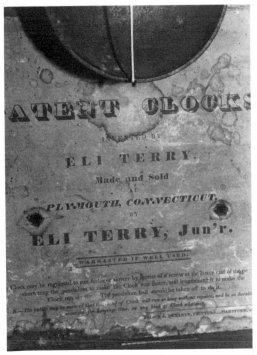

Label from Eli Terry, Jr., mahogany-veneered shelf clock.

Seth Thomas Plymouth Hollow, Connecticut, mahogany-veneered shelf clock with ebony and gold-leaf painted columns; 30-hour, time and strike, weight driven, brass movement patented 1867 (may not be the original movement); 18¼″ wide, 32½″ high; **$600.**

Seth Thomas mahogany-veneered shelf clock with artificially grained pillars, circa 1855–59; 8-day, time and strike, weight driven; 16½″ wide, 32¼″ high; **$300.**

OG (ogee) Clocks

Seth Thomas miniature ogee mahogany shelf clock, after 1865; 30-hour, time, strike, and alarm; 10" wide, 16" high; **$100.**

Seth Thomas miniature ogee mahogany shelf clock, after 1865; 30-hour, time and strike; 11" wide, 16½" high; **$140.**

Seth Thomas miniature ogee rosewood shelf clock, after 1865; 30-hour, time and strike, spring driven; 10½" wide, 16½" high; **$275.** E. N. Welch ogee rosewood shelf clock, circa 1850; 8-day time and strike, spring driven; 11½" wide, 18½" high; **$350.**

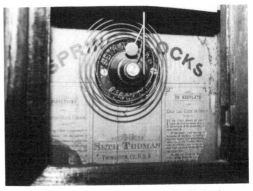

Label from Seth Thomas ogee shelf clock.

Seth Thomas miniature ogee mahogany simple calendar shelf clock with Seem's dial patented January 7, 1868; 30-hour, time and strike, spring driven; 12" wide, 18" high; no price available. Seth Thomas mirror ogee mahogany simple calendar shelf clock with Seem's dial patented January 7, 1868; 30-hour, time and strike, weight driven; 15½" wide, 26" high; no price available.

Closeup of dial from Seth Thomas simple calendar shelf clock, marked "Seem's dial Patented January 7, 1868."

Label from Seth Thomas simple calendar shelf clock.

Seem's label from Seth Thomas simple calendar shelf clock.

4
Wall Clocks

Did You Know?

Victorian features such as carvings, heads, upright and drop finials, and curved moldings decorated wall-clock cases made in the latter half of the 1800s. Incised carving prevailed around 1870.

Walnut was the predominate wood used in the manufacture of clocks during the latter half of the 1800s.

The bobs on pendulum rods varied. The bobs were usually round, but some were engraved or embossed or had leaf appendages. Some featured a man's head in low relief or female portraits. Others were geometrical in design, or had similar creative features. Bobs were available in crystal, sandwich glass (made in layers), and wood. Some were cylindrical, such as the silver-colored ones made to imitate mercury. The French mercury pendulums were genuine, while those made in America were imitation.

Octagon clocks are frequently referred to as schoolhouse clocks. They were also popular in offices and churches.

Gallery clocks were designed for use in public places, where their large, round dials could readily be seen. Either 8-day or electric, they have been made since 1845 until the present.

Papier-mâché advertising clocks containing Seth Thomas movements were made by Edward P. Baird of Plattsburgh, New York, from 1890 to 1896. Later, in Evanston, Illinois, from around 1896 to 1900, Baird made wooden clocks with embossed or painted messages rimming a metal dial.

The Sidney Advertiser Clock, Sidney, New York, circa 1885, had a bell that rang and advertising drums that turned every five minutes. Complete clocks are not easy to find, but reproduction drums are available.

Hanging shelf clocks have self-contained shelves that look like they are sitting on shelves when they are actually hanging on the wall.

Gustav Stickley's Mission style was characterized by straight, strong, stoic oak furniture and accessories, including clocks. It was in vogue until 1920 and again in the 1960s.

The first calendar movement appeared on an English tall-case clock around 1660. The first known American patent for a simple calendar-clock mechanism was issued to J. H. Hawes of Ithaca, New York, in 1853.

A perpetual calendar clock shows the day of the week, the month, and the date and is self-adjusting to allow for leap years.

A simple calendar clock needs an occasional manual adjustment to make it totally accurate.

Regulators

Ansonia Brass & Copper Company rosewood round-top, short-drop wall clock, circa 1854–59; 8-day, time and strike, spring driven; 24" high, 11" dial; **$375.**

E. Ingraham Company walnut ionic round-top, round-drop wall clock, circa 1875; 8-day, time and strike, spring driven; 22" high, lower glass diameter 6", 10" dial; **$285.**

E. N. Welch rosewood round-top, long-drop wall clock; 8-day, time only, with two keyholes to wind weights; 35" high; 11½" dial; **$775.**

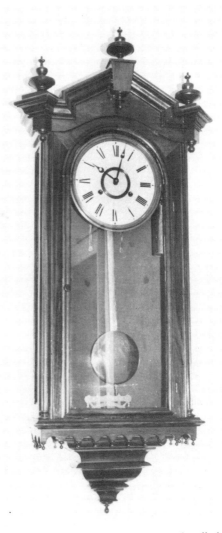

Welch & Spring Company rosewood wall clock, circa 1868–84; 8-day, time and strike, weight driven; 15" wide, 40" high; **$1,200.**

Waterbury "Halifax" oak wall clock, circa 1880; 8-day, time and strike, spring driven; 10" wide, 33" high; **$600.** *New Haven "Pacific" oak wall clock, circa 1880; 8-day, time only, spring driven; 16¾" wide, 38" high;* **$300.**

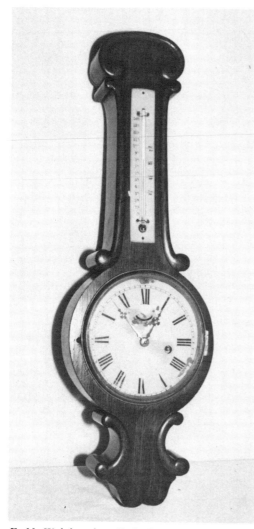

E. N. Welch oak wall clock with thermometer, circa 1880; 8-day, time only, lever movement; 23" high, 5½" dial; **$175.**

Waterbury "Library" mahogany wall clock, circa 1860, with porcelain dial; 8-day, time and strike with chains that pull up weights; 17½" wide, 41" high, porcelain dial; **$1,000.**

F. Kroeber "Scythia" ebony-finished wall clock with beveled mirror at base, circa 1884; 8-day, time and strike, spring driven; 9¾" wide, 27" high, porcelain dial; **$700.** *F. Kroeber "Reflector," ebony-finished wall clock with mirrors at sides, a drawer at base, open escapement and porcelain dial, patented date March 7, 1884, on pendulum; 8-day, time and strike, spring driven; 13" wide, 32" high, porcelain dial;* **$1,000.**

E. Howard & Company "Model 75" walnut wall clock, circa 1875–80; 8-day, time only, weight driven; 9¾" wide at base, 15¼" wide at top, 33" high, 11½" dial; **$3,000.**

Waterbury "Halifax" oak wall clock, circa 1880–90; 8-day, time and strike, spring driven; 10" wide, 33" high, 5½" dial; **$300.** *Waterbury two-weight open swinger oak wall clock, circa 1880–90; 8-day, time only; 17" wide, 30" high, 8" dial;* **$700.**

Self Winding Clock Company battery-operated oak wall clock; time only; 19¼" wide, 30" high, 7" dial; **$375.**

Waterbury walnut short-drop wall clock, circa 1880–90; time only, spring driven; 15" wide, 25" high; **$325.**

Ansonia "Charlotte" oak wall clock; 8-day, time and strike, spring driven; 16" wide, 41" high; **$700.**

Seth Thomas mahogany wall clock, circa 1900; 30-day, time and strike, spring driven; 19½" wide, 30" high, 7" dial; **$550.**

W. L. Gilbert Clock Company "Number 11 Regulator" walnut wall clock, circa 1888; 8-day, time and strike, weight driven with keyhole on right that winds both weights on same drum; 14½" wide, 50" high, 7" dial;; **$1,250.**

Ansonia "Capitol" walnut wall clock; 8-day, time and strike, spring driven; 13¾" wide, 53" high, 7" dial; **$1,200.**

E. N. Welch walnut hanging shelf clock, circa 1880; 8-day, time and strike, alarm, spring driven; 13½" wide, 26" high; **$325.**

Seth Thomas walnut hanging shelf clock; 8-day, time, strike, and alarm, spring driven; 15" wide, 27" high; **$525.**

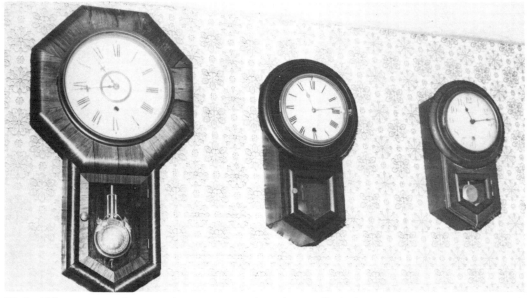

W. L. Gilbert rosewood-veneered octagon top, short-drop wall clock; 8-day, time only; 21" high, 7½" dial; **$150;** *New Haven pine stained (probably a salesman's sample) round-top, short-drop wall clock; 8-day, time only; 14½" high, 4½" dial;* **$150;** *Waterbury green painted (probably a salesman's sample) round-top, short-drop wall clock; 8-day, time only; 13" high, 5" dial;* **$150.**

New Haven works in English walnut case with marquetry designs; 8-day, time and strike, spring driven; 38" high, $7\frac{1}{2}$" dial; **$625.**

Waterbury "Number 53" walnut wall clock, circa 1900; 8-day, time only, weight driven; 20" wide at top, $53\frac{1}{4}$" high, 9" dial; **$1,300.**

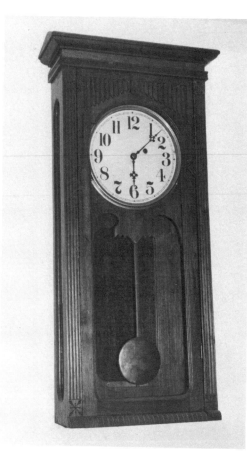

W. L. Gilbert walnut wall clock with pediment missing, circa 1890; 8-day, time only, weight driven; 15½" wide, 37" high, 9½" dial; **$425.**

W. L. Gilbert "Shield" walnut wall clock, circa 1881; 8-day, time and strike, spring driven; 10½" wide, 29" high, 6" dial; **$600.**

Waterbury "Saranac" oak hanging shelf clock, circa 1880; 8-day, time and strike, spring driven; 13¼" wide, 31" high, 5" dial; **$200;** *E. Ingraham "Mount Vernon" oak hanging shelf clock, circa 1880; 8-day, time and strike, spring driven; 14½" wide, 27" high, 5" dial;* **$200.**

Sessions oak wall clock, circa 1903; 8-day, time and strike, weight driven with narrow flat weights to make them more undiscernable; 17" wide, 64" high, 11" dial; **$1,200.**

W. L. Gilbert "Number 10½" oak wall clock; 8-day, time only, weight driven; 16" wide, 53" high; **$1,500.**

George B. Owen Clock Company, New York, walnut wall clock, circa 1854; 8-day, time and bell strike; 13" wide, 36" high, 7½" dial; **$500.**

W. L. Gilbert "Gladstone" walnut wall clock; 8-day, time only, spring driven; 13" wide, 38" high, 7" dial; **$400.**

Sessions oak wall clock, circa 1903; 8-day, time and strike, weight driven; 52" high, 12" dial; **$800.**

American Clock Company battery-operated birch wall clock; time only; 16" wide, 47" high, 11" dial; **$500.**

51

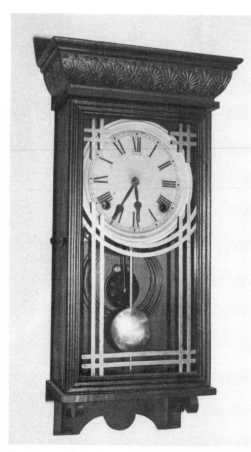

Sessions wall clock; 8-day, time and strike, spring driven; 19" high, 5" dial; **$175.**

E. N. Welch "Italian" rosewood hanging shelf clock (new, exact copy case but with original movement); 8-day, time and strike, spring driven; 15" wide, 29" high, 6" dial; **$700** *for exact copy;* **$1,500** *for original clock.*

W. L. Gilbert stained walnut wall clock; 30-hour, time and strike, weight driven; 16" wide, 47" high; $250.

Waterbury "Elgin" oak wall clock; 8-day, time only, spring driven; 15" wide, 33½" high; $600.

Seth Thomas, "Number 1 Extra" Plymouth Hollow, Connecticut, rosewood parlor wall regulator, circa 1860; 8-day, time and strike, weight driven; 41" high, 13½" dial; **$1,200.**

Seth Thomas pine round-top, long-drop regulator; 8-day, time only, weight driven; 33" high, 12" dial; **$800.**

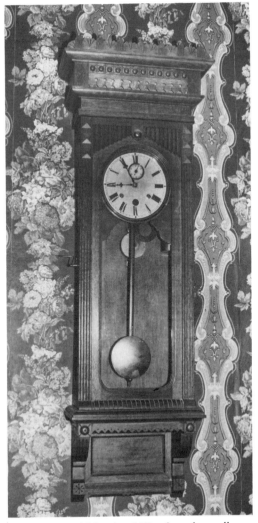

W. L. Gilbert "Number 10" walnut parlor wall regulator, circa 1888; 8-day, time only, weight driven; 17½" wide, 54" high; **$1,500.**

W. L. Gilbert "Number 11" ash parlor wall regulator, circa 1888; 8-day, time and strike, weight driven; 15" wide, 50" high, 8" dial; **$1,500.**

New Haven mahogany round-top, long-drop regulator; 8-day, time only, spring driven; 32" high, 12" dial; **$375.**

Chelsea "Number 1" oak round-top, long-drop regulator, circa 1897; 8-day, time only, weight driven; 10½" wide, 32" high, 12" dial; **$975.**

New Haven oak wall regulator, early 1900's; 8-day, time and strike, spring driven; 16" wide, 35" high; **$425.**

New Haven walnut round-top, short-drop regulator; 8-day, time and strike, spring driven; 16" wide, 28" high; **$395.**

W. L. Gilbert "Number 14" oak parlor wall regulator; 8-day, time only, weight driven; 17" wide, 49" high; **$1,500.**

Seth Thomas "Number 2" walnut round-top, long-drop regulator, circa 1888; 8-day, time only, weight driven; 34" high, 12" dial; **$900.**

Waterbury "Number 3" walnut parlor wall regulator; 8-day, time only, weight driven; 16" wide, 45" high, 8" dial; **$1,400.**

Sessions oak parlor wall regulator, circa 1903; 8-day, time only, spring driven; 17" wide, 35" high; **$350.**

W. L. Gilbert oak parlor wall regulator; time only; 13½" wide, 36" high; **$395.**

E. N. Welch "Number 2" rosewood round-top, long-drop regulator, with exact-copy case and old works; 8-day, time only, weight driven; 16" wide, 55" high, 18" dial; **$2,000** *for exact-copy case and original works;* **$4,000** *for original clock.*

New Haven oak parlor wall regulator, early 1900s; 30-hour, time only, spring driven; 16" wide, 45" high; **$400.**

W. L. Gilbert oak "Number 12" jeweler's wall regulator, early 1900s; 8-day, time only, weight driven; 30" wide, 84" high; **$4,200.**

New Haven "Number 2" oak round-top, long-drop regulator, circa 1900; 30-day, time and strike; 35" high, 11½" dial; **$475.**

Seth Thomas "Number 2" walnut round-top, long-drop regulator; 8-day, time only, weight driven; 10" wide, 35" high, 11¼" dial; **$650.**

Octagons

E. Ingraham octagon-top, short-drop regulator, early 1900s; 8-day, time only, spring driven; 24½" high, 11¼" dial; **$250.**

E. N. Welch ''Verdi'' rosewood octagon, long-drop wall clock, circa 1875; 8-day, time and strike, spring driven; 31" high, 11½" dial; **$450.**

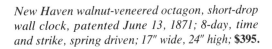

New Haven walnut-veneered octagon, short-drop wall clock, patented June 13, 1871; 8-day, time and strike, spring driven; 17" wide, 24" high; **$395.**

E. N. Welch mahogany-veneered octagon, short-drop wall clock; 8-day, time only, spring driven; 26" high, 11½" dial; **$250.**

E. N. Welch "Number 2" mahogany-veneered octagon, short-drop wall clock, circa 1880; 8-day, time only, spring driven; 17" wide, 25½" high; **$295.**

E. Ingraham oak octagon, short-drop wall clock; 8-day, time only, spring driven, 18" wide, 24" high; **$325.**

Waterbury "Yeddo" rosewood-veneered octagon, short-drop wall clock with brass trim, circa 1900; 8-day, time and strike, spring driven; 21" high, 10" dial; **$250.**

Seth Thomas oak octagon, short-drop wall clock, with label reading "Union Pacific Railroad Company Station Clock"; 8-day, time only, spring driven; 24" high; **$375.**

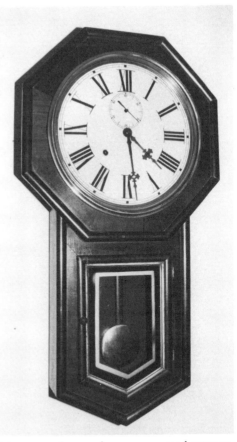

Unknown maker, mahogany-veneered octagon, long-drop wall clock; 8-day, time and strike, spring driven; 31¼" high, 12" dial; **$425.**

Seth Thomas oak octagon, short-drop wall clock; 8-day, time only, spring driven; 17½" high, 8" dial; **$175.**

Ball Watch Company, Cleveland, oak octagon, short-drop wall clock, circa 1880; 8-day, time only, spring driven; 24" high, 12" dial; **$285.**

Seth Thomas walnut octagon, short-drop wall clock, circa 1900; 8-day, time only, spring driven; 21½" high; **$325.**

Waterbury "Yeddo" rosewood-veneered octagon, short-drop wall clock with brass trim, circa 1900; 8-day, time and strike, spring driven; 14" wide, 21½" high, 10" dial; **$275.**

Waterbury octagon, short-drop wall clock, circa 1900; 8-day, time only, spring driven; 19" high, 7" dial; **$350.**

Sessions oak octagon, short-drop wall clock, circa 1903; 8-day, time only, spring driven; 24" high, 10" dial; **$225.**

Gallery Clocks

E. Ingraham gallery clock, circa 1900; time only, spring driven; 16" diameter; **$175.**

Waterbury oak gallery clock; 30-day, time only, spring driven; 30" diameter, 23" dial; **$500.**

Seth Thomas metal-case gallery clock; 30-day, time only, spring driven; 22" diameter, 13" dial; **$150.**

Seth Thomas oak gallery clock; 30-day, time only; 20" diameter, 17" dial; **$200.**

Advertising Clocks

Baird Advertiser, Plattsburgh, New York, papier-mâché-case wall clock, with movement by Seth Thomas, circa 1890; 8-day, time only, spring driven; 18½" wide, 30½" high; **$1,200.**

Sidney Advertiser, Sidney, New York, oak calendar wall clock, with movement by Seth Thomas; repainted tablet and replaced exact copies of advertising drums; 8-day, time only, spring driven; 28" wide, 72" high; **$4,000.**

Waterbury oak round-top, short-drop jeweler's wall clock; 8-day, time only, spring driven; 24" high, 11" dial; **$200.**

E. Ingraham oak advertising wall clock, circa 1900; 8-day, time only; 17" wide, 38" high; **$395.**

Waterbury "Orient" square-top, short-drop jeweler's wall clock; 8-day, time only, spring driven; 10" wide at base, 15" wide at top, 27" high, 9" dial; no price available.

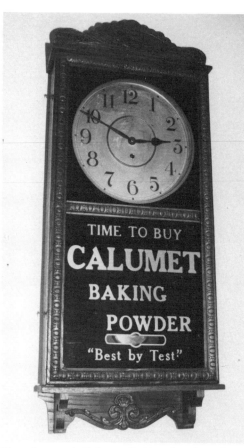

Waterbury oak octagon, short-drop advertising wall clock with reversed dial and hands that turn counterclockwise; often used in barbershops to reflect time in mirror; 8-day, time only, spring driven; 23" high, 11" dial; **$300.**

Waterbury oak Calumet Baking Powder advertising wall clock with repainted tablet; 8-day, time only, spring driven; 16" wide, 38" high; **$425.**

Hammond Clock Company metal-case Postal Telegraph "Synchronous Electric Time" gallery wall clock, circa 1931; 15" dial; **$75.**

Mission-Style Clocks

Sessions walnut-stained La Reforma advertising wall clock with repainted tablet, circa 1903; 8-day, time only, spring driven; 16½" wide, 38" high; **$425.**

Unknown maker, Mission-style oak wall clock; 8-day, time and strike, spring driven; 12¾" wide, 26" high; **$125.**

W. L. Gilbert Mission-style oak shelf clock with slag glass flanking dial, dated 1913 on works; 8-day, time and strike, spring driven; 20" wide, 6" deep, 13" high; **$145.**

Ingraham miniature oak Mission shelf clock, with brass hands and numbers on dial; 8-day, time only, spring driven; 6" wide, 14¾" high; **$200.**

Unknown maker, Mission-style oak wall clock; 8-day, time and strike, spring driven; 12½" square; **$85.**

Calendar Clocks

The Prentiss Clock Company, New York, mahogany wall-hanging calendar clock, circa 1890; 60-day, time only, double spring movement and spring-driven calendar that only needs to be wound once a year; 12" wide, 36" high, 9½" dial; **$2,500.**

L. F. & W. W. Carter, Bristol, Connecticut, rosewood wall-hanging perpetual calendar clock with double dial, circa 1863–68; 8-day, time only, weight driven; 22" wide, 59" high, top dial 17½", bottom dial 11½"; **$1,800.**

Ithaca "Cottage" walnut wall-hanging calendar clock with double dial, H. B. Horton's calendar patents, April 18, 1865, and August 28, 1866; 8-day, time and strike, spring driven; 12" wide, 25" high, 5" upper dial, 7" lower dial; **$925.**

Macomb Clock Company walnut wall-hanging perpetual calendar clock with double-dial Seem's calendar and 8 phases of the moon and movement by E. N. Welch, circa 1882–83; 8-day, time and strike, spring driven; 14½" wide, 30" high, 6" dial; no price available.

Seth Thomas "Number 6½" rosewood-veneered wall-hanging double-dial perpetual calendar clock, with calendar movement patented February 15, 1876; 8-day, time only, spring driven; 32" high, 11½" top dial, 9½" bottom dial; **$700;** *New Haven "Register" walnut wall-hanging double-dial perpetual calendar clock; 8-day, time only, spring driven; 12" wide, 33" high, 7" top dial, 7½" bottom dial;* **$600.**

New Haven oak wall-hanging simple calendar clock with double dial; 30-day, time only, spring driven; 19½" wide, 48" high; **$1,200.**

E. N. Welch "Damrosch" walnut wall-hanging perpetual calendar clock with double dial; 8-day, time only, spring driven; 14" wide, 41" high, 8" dials; **$1,900.**

E. N. Welch walnut wall-hanging perpetual calendar clock; an exact copy of case and dials but with original works; Daniel J. Gale Astronomical Calendar clock patents, 1871, 1877, and 1885; 8-day, time and strike, spring driven; 17" wide, 30" high, 11" dial; **$1,500** for exact copy, **$3,000** for original clock.

E. Ingraham stained walnut round-top, round-drop wall-hanging simple calendar clock, circa 1890; 8-day, time only, spring driven; 24" high, 11" dial; **$350.**

Ansonia Brass & Copper Company rosewood-veneered round-top, short-drop wall-hanging perpetual calendar clock with W. A. Terry's calendar movement patents, 1868, 1870, and 1875; an exact copy of case and dial but with original works; 8-day, time and strike; 16" wide, 25½" high, 11" dial; **$350** for exact copy, **$700** for original clock.

*E. N. Welch "Number 1" rosewood-veneered wall-hanging calendar clock with double dial; an exact copy of case and dials but with original works; 8-day, time only; 16½" wide, 54½" high; **$1,000** for exact copy, **$2,700** for original clock.*

*E. Ingraham oak wall-hanging simple calendar clock; 8-day, time only, spring driven; 16" wide, 36" high, 11" dial; **$250.***

Ansonia Brass and Copper Company "Novelty Calendar" mahogany-veneered octagon, short-drop simple calendar clock; an exact-copy case; 8-day, time only, spring driven; 17" wide, 26" high, 10¾" dial; **$250** *for exact copy,* **$500** *for original clock.*

W. L. Gilbert walnut round-top, short-drop wall-hanging simple calendar clock, early 1900s; 8-day, time and strike, spring driven; 18¼" wide, 31" high; **$650.**

W. L. Gilbert walnut round-top, short-drop wall-hanging simple calendar clock with G. Maranville's calendar movement patent 1861; 8-day, time only, spring driven; 17½" wide, 33½" high, 14½" dial; **$800.**

W. L. Gilbert "Berkshire" walnut wall-hanging simple calendar clock, circa 1870; 8-day, time and strike, spring driven; 14½" wide, 38" high, 8" dial; **$3,500.**

Welch, Spring & Company "Calendar Number 1" rosewood round-top, long-drop, wall-hanging double-dial calendar clock, circa 1868–84, with B. B. Lewis-type calendar dial; 8-day, time only, weight driven; 18" wide, 52½" high; **$1,500.**

Sessions oak wall-hanging calendar clock, circa 1910–20; 8-day, time only, spring driven; 16¾" wide, 38" high; **$500.**

E. N. Welch oak-veneered octagon, short-drop simple calendar clock, dated 1887; 8-day, time and strike, spring driven; 17" wide, 24" high; **$495.**

Ansonia Brass and Copper Company "Novelty Calendar" mahogany-veneered octagon, short-drop simple calendar clock; 8-day, time only, spring driven; 17" wide, 26" high, 10½" dial; **$1,000.**

Terry Clock Company walnut octagon, short-drop simple calendar clock; 8-day, time only, spring driven; 14½" wide, 22½" high, 9" dial; **$200.**

Sessions oak wall-hanging calendar clock, early 1900s, 8-day, time only, spring driven; 16¾" wide, 36" high; **$495.**

William M. Wrigley Clock Company, "Chicago" marked on movement, oak octagon, short-drop simple calendar clock; 8-day, time only, spring driven; 17" wide, 24" high; **$465.**

81

L. F. & W. W. Carter Clock Company, Bristol, Connecticut, rosewood round-top, short-drop perpetual calendar clock with double dial, circa 1863–68; 8-day, time and strike, spring driven; 32" high, 11½" dial; **$1,050.**

Ithaca "Number 4" walnut wall-hanging perpetual calendar clock with H. B. Horton's perpetual calendar movement patent 1865; 8-day, time and strike, double spring driven; 31" high, 12" diameter upper dial, 9" diameter lower dial; **$1,200.**

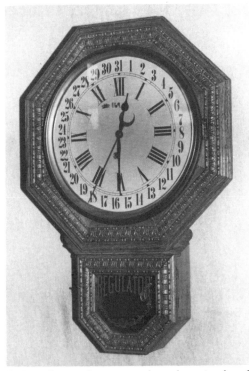

*E. Ingraham oak octagon, short-drop simple cal-
endar clock, circa 1900; 8-day, time only, spring
driven; 17" wide, 24" high;* **$395.**

5
Shelf Clocks

Did You Know?

The design of the steeple clock with a pointed Gothic feel is credited to Elias Ingraham of Bristol, Connecticut. Some have two steeples and others have four. They were made around 1840, when brass-coiled springs were available, and are still being produced today.

A beehive clock has a rounded Gothic arch that resembles its namesake. It was made in the late 1840s and production continued until the early 1900s.

Hundreds of different stencils were used to paint clock tablets through the 1850s. Etched glass tablets appeared after 1840. Decalcomania transfers were common on clock tablets in the late 1800s but are not considered as desirable as the early reverse-painted ones.

The tambour clock was also called "hunchback" or "camelback." This round-top shelf clock was made around 1900 and is still being produced today.

In the 1880s Seth Thomas sold bronze statuettes for clocks to other manufacturers. New figures can be purchased to replace those missing from old clocks. Hands, dials, and finials are also available. Collectors sometimes replace dials, but they retain the originals to keep the clocks authentic. Purists keep their clocks in their original condition without making any additions or changes.

The Ansonia Clock Company in 1889 offered an assortment of three oak shelf clocks—the "Gallatin," the "Echo," and the "Griswold"—for $12.60. They were 8-day clocks with a gong strike and listed as "Sure Sellers, Big Money-Makers."

Ansonia's 1893 Bankers Assortment of six clocks for $12.50 featured three walnut clocks

New Haven mahogany shelf clock with inlay on case; 8-day, time only, spring driven; 14¼" wide, 6½" high; **$45.** *Seth Thomas wooden beehive shelf clock; 8-day, time only, spring driven; 4½" wide, 6½" high;* **$45.** *Seth Thomas mahogany shelf clock; 30-hour, time and alarm; 4½" wide, 4" high;* **$40.**

Seth Thomas mahogany tambour shelf clock; 8-day, time only, spring driven; 18" wide, 9½" high; **$150.** *Seth Thomas "Camden" black-enameled wooden-case tambour shelf clock; 8-day, time only, spring driven;* **$95.**

---

called "Berkely," "Buffalo," and "Beaver" and three oak cases labeled "Belmont," "Bedford," and "Burton." All were 8-day, strike clocks and two had alarms. As an added incentive, no charge was added for the shipping case. Today's cost would be about $1,200.

A rotary press was used to force a design into wooden clock cases after they had been softened with steam. These "pressed" designs, as they are currently known, resemble carvings.

Oak shelf clocks were popular from about 1880 to about 1915. Many were called kitchen clocks.

Samuel Emerson Root metal wall clock with case made by Nicholas Muller, circa 1850; 8-day, time only, marine movement; 12" diameter, 5" dial; no price available.

Chauncey Jerome ebonized shelf clock, with mother-of-pearl decorations, circa 1845–55; 8-day, time and strike, fusee spring driven; 12" wide, 17" high; **$200.**

Some clocks appeared in series, including cities, rivers, and historic places such as Mt. Vernon or the Capitol Dome. E. Ingraham's Army-Navy series featured President McKinley, Admiral Dewey, Robert E. Lee, the battleship ''Maine,'' a Peace dove, and an Emblem. E. N. Welch made a series of the 1898 Spanish-American War leaders. The figures in both series were pressed into the wood. Tablets were stenciled with ships, flags, or similar themes.

Samuel Emerson Root was one of the first makers of marine movements in America. He was at work in Bristol, Connecticut, in 1851. One of his clocks is pictured in this chapter under metal clocks. Root did not ordinarily make clocks, so this signed example is a rare one. It has a metal case made by Nicholas Muller of New York City.

Marine or lever clocks operate with a hairspring balance. As opposed to a pendulum clock, these clocks continue to run even when being transported or when placed on uneven surfaces. Marine or lever clocks were mass-produced in the 1850s. They can be used anywhere, including aboard ships. In

Label from Chauncey Jerome fusee shelf clock.

the 1890s, this movement was used in alarm clocks.

Iron-front and cast-iron clock cases were made by Nicholas Muller in his foundry in New York City around 1850. Nicholas Muller's Sons produced bronze- and iron-case shelf clocks around 1880.

The reported earnings for a skilled mechanic in an 1880 clock factory was $3.00 for a ten-hour day. The common laborer earned $1.50 a day. Men, women, and children worked side by side.

Black mantel clocks, popular from 1880 to 1920, were made of marble, black-painted metal, or black enameled wood. Adamantine, a patented, colored celluloid veneer, was used on clock cases to imitate onyx, marble, and other finishes.

Two black parlor clocks are described in the 1897 Sears, Roebuck Catalogue. One is listed as "Fresno with a very fine polished wood case in imitation of black onyx, fancy gilt engraving, marbleized columns, with gilt bronze bases and caps . . ." while the other is listed as "Colusa with a fine polished wood case, in imitation of marble, with fancy gilt bronze side ornaments."

The 1908 Sears, Roebuck Catalogue featured black enameled wood clocks and described one as "finished to imitate black Italian marble and green Mexican onyx."

Keeping imitation clock finishes new can be achieved by rubbing a woolen cloth slightly sprinkled with sweet oil over the surfaces. This is a suggestion from an early Sears catalogue.

"Higher sprier" and "lower slower" is a good way to remember that raising the bob on the pendulum rod shortens the pendulum's swing so the clock goes faster. Lowering it makes the arc wider and slows the clock's speed.

Bedroom clocks were time only because striking noises might awaken a sleeper.

Round alarm clocks have been manufactured since the 1880s. The Western Clock Manufacturing Company was established in La Salle, Illinois, in 1895. Its "Big Ben" alarm came out in 1910. "Little Ben" appeared five years later. Westclox, a trade name, became the company name in 1936.

Celluloid, an early plastic, was patented in 1869.

Calendar Clocks

Seth Thomas ''Number Three'' rosewood double-dial perpetual calendar shelf clocks, left clock patented February 15, 1876, right clock patented January 31, 1860; 8-day, time and strike, spring driven; 13¾" wide, 27" high, 7½" dials; $500 each.

Jerome oak double-dial perpetual calendar shelf clock, circa 1850; an exact copy of case and calendar movement; 8-day, time and strike, spring driven; 10½" wide, 21½" high, 3½" top dial, 4½" bottom dial; $500 for exact copy, $1,000 for original clock.

Macomb Calendar Clock Company ''Kokomo'' walnut calendar shelf clock, circa 1882–83; 8-day, time and strike, spring driven; 16¾" wide, 28" high, 6" dial; $4,000. Macomb Calendar Clock Company walnut calendar shelf clock, circa 1882–83; 8-day, time and strike, spring driven; 15½" wide, 28" high, 6" dial; $4,000. Both clocks have original cases and works but with new moon dials and missing calendars at base.

Closeup of Macomb Calendar Clock Manufacturing Company imprint on clock mechanism.

89

Seth Thomas "Calendar Number 10" walnut double-dial calendar shelf clock with R. T. Andrew's February 15, 1876, patent calendar movement; 8-day, time and strike, weight driven; 22" wide, 36½" high, 9½" dials; no price available.

Ithaca walnut double-dial calendar shelf clock with H. B. Horton's August 28, 1866, patent calendar movement; 8-day, time and strike, spring driven; 12" wide, 25" high, 5½" upper dial, 7" lower dial; **$650.** *Ithaca walnut double-dial calendar shelf clock with H. B. Horton's August 28, 1866, patent calendar movement; an exact copy of case and dials but with original movement; 8-day, time and strike, spring driven; 10" wide, 20" high, 5" upper dial, 7" lower dial;* **$1,500** *for exact copy,* **$2,500** *for original clock.*

Waterbury "Buffalo" walnut simple calendar shelf clock, late 1800s; 8-day, time and strike, spring driven; 17½" wide, 27" high, 7" dial; **$300.** *Waterbury "Number 38 Calendar" walnut double-dial perpetual calendar shelf clock; 8-day, time only, spring driven; 13½" wide, 26" high, 5" dials;* **$600.**

Waterbury "Oswego" oak double-dial, perpetual calendar shelf clock with A. F. Wells's July 30, 1889, patent calendar movement; 8-day, time and strike, spring driven; 17" wide, 28" high, 7" dial, $650. Waterbury "Number 43 Calendar" oak double-dial, perpetual calendar shelf clock, with A. F. Wells's July 30, 1889, patent calendar movement; 8-day, time and strike, spring driven; 16" wide, 29" high, 7" dials; $650.

Seth Thomas "Number 5" walnut double-dial calendar shelf clock with R. T. Andrew's February 15, 1876, patent calendar movement; 8-day, time and strike, spring driven; 12½" wide, 20" high, 7" dials; $835.

New Haven "Monarch" oak double-dial simple calendar shelf clock; 8-day, time and strike, spring driven; 15" wide, 27" high, 5" dials; $600. E. N. Welch "Italian" round-top double-dial perpetual calendar shelf clock; 8-day, time and strike, spring driven; 12" wide, 20" high, 6½" dials; $500.

Closeup of label from New Haven double-dial simple calendar shelf clock.

Closeup of roller-type calendar movement on Waterbury simple calendar shelf clock.

Waterbury walnut simple calendar shelf clock, circa 1890, with roller-type calendar movement; 8-day, time only, spring driven; 13¾" wide, 32" high, 7" dial; **$1,500.**

W. L. Gilbert rosewood simple calendar shelf clock with G. B. Owen's April 24, 1886, patent calendar movement; 8-day, time and strike, spring driven; 10" wide, 13" high, 5" dial; **$700.** *W. L. Gilbert walnut simple calendar shelf clock with moon phase; 8-day, time and strike, spring driven; 11½" wide, 19" high, 5" dial;* **$600.**

E. N. Welch walnut perpetual calendar shelf clock with Franklin-Morse's June 12, 1883, patent calendar movement; 8-day, time and strike, spring driven; 16" wide, 22½" high, 5" dial; **$650.** *Waterbury walnut double-dial, perpetual calendar shelf clock with C. W. Feishtinger's October 9, 1894, patent calendar movement; 8-day, time and strike, spring driven; 13" wide, 22" high, 5" dials;* **$650.**

Waterbury mahogany-veneered calendar shelf clock with Seem's dial, patent January 7, 1868; 8-day, time and strike, spring driven; 11" wide, 16½" high; **$700.**

New Haven oak simple calendar shelf clock, circa 1885; 8-day, time and strike, spring driven; 15" wide, 25" high; **$275.**

W. L. Gilbert "Elberon" oak simple (the month disk must be moved manually) calendar shelf clock with McCabe's November 10, 1896, patent calendar movement; repainted tablet has flowers instead of birds; this clock was sold by the Southern Calendar Clock Company in the late 1890s; 8-day, time and strike, spring driven; 15" wide, 30½" high, 8" dial; **$1,700.**

Waterbury walnut double-dial perpetual calendar shelf clock, A. F. Wells's July 30, 1889, patent calendar movement; 8-day, time and strike, spring driven; 16½" wide, 29" high, 7" dials; **$1,200.**

Seth Thomas walnut double-dial calendar shelf clock, circa 1876; 8-day, time and strike, spring driven; 16" wide, 32" high, 8" dials; **$1,500.**

E. N. Welch walnut double-dial, perpetual calendar shelf clock, circa 1889; an exact copy of case but with old works; 8-day, time and strike, spring driven; 20" wide, 31½" high, 7" dials; **$900** *for exact copy,* **$1,800** *for original clock.*

E. N. Welch "Arditi" walnut double-dial, per-petual calendar shelf clock with D. J. Gale's April 21, 1885, patent calendar movement; 8-day, time and strike, spring driven; $17\frac{1}{2}''$ wide, $27\frac{1}{2}''$ high, 7" dials; **$1,800.**

Parker Clock Company, miniature brass simple calendar shelf clock, patented March 14, 1882; 30-hour, time only, spring driven; 5" wide, $8\frac{1}{2}''$ high; **$500.**

Steeple Clocks

Burroughs Clock Company, Lowell, Massachusetts, mahogany-veneered, miniature steeple clock, circa 1870–74; 4¾" wide, 7" high, **$100;** *Marlow & Company, York, Pennsylvania, mahogany-veneered ogee box clock (miniature reproduction) copied from Jerome & Darrow's box clock made between 1824 and 1831, circa 1870; 3¼" wide, 5¾" high;* **$100;** *Burroughs Clock Company cherry, miniature rounded steeple or onion-top clock, circa 1870–74; 5" wide, 7" high;* **$100.**

New Haven "Jerome" rosewood steeple clock; 8-day, time and strike, spring driven; 10" wide, 19" high, 4½" dial; **$150.** *W. L. Gilbert rosewood steeple clock; 30-hour, time and strike, spring driven; 11" wide, 20" high;* **$150.**

W. L. Gilbert mahoany-veneered steeple clock, circa 1870; 30-hour, time and strike, spring driven; **$165.**

New Haven oak steeple clock; 8-day, time and strike, spring driven; 9½" wide, 15½" high; **$125.** *W. L. Gilbert mahogany-veneered steeple clock; 8-day, time and strike; spring driven; 9¼" wide, 16" high;* **$125.**

New Haven miniature rosewood steeple clock with reverse painting on tablet; 30-hour, time and strike, spring driven; 7½" wide, 14½" high; **$200.**

J. C. Brown & Company rosewood steeple clock, circa 1842–49; 8-day, time and strike, spring driven; 10" wide, 20" high; **$300.**

Ansonia Brass & Copper Company, mahogany-veneered steeple clock, circa 1854–79; 8-day, time and strike, alarm, spring driven; 11" wide, 20" high, 4¼" dial; **$245.**

Parlor Clocks

Seth Thomas walnut shelf clock; 30-hour, time, strike, and alarm, spring driven; 12" wide, 15½" high; **$145.** *E. N. Welch mahogany shelf clock, patented 1868; 30-hour, time and strike, spring driven; 10½" wide, 14" high;* **$145.**

Seth Thomas rosewood shelf (bedroom) clock, circa 1855; 30-hour, time only and alarm, spring driven; 7½" wide, 9½" high; **$165.**

New Haven rosewood-veneered shelf clock; 30-hour, time, strike, and alarm, spring driven; 9½" wide, 13½" high; **$195.**

Birge & Mallory mahogany beehive shelf clock with a J. Ives patented movement, circa 1838–43; 8-day, time and strike, wagon-spring driven; 14" wide, 26½" high; **$2,500.**

E. N. Welch "Iowa Model" walnut shelf clock with imitation mercury pendulum; 8-day, time and strike, spring driven; 16" wide, 24" high; **$500.**

New Haven "Corsair" oak shelf clock; 8-day, time, strike, and alarm, spring driven; 17" wide, 23½" high, 5" dial; $500.

Ansonia walnut-stained case with hand-painted leather panels, open escapement; 8-day, time and strike; 16" wide, 17½" high; $385.

E. N. Welch "Lucca" rosewood shelf clock, circa 1870; 8-day, time and strike, spring driven; 14" wide, 23" high; $600.

W. L. Gilbert walnut shelf clock, circa 1870; 8-day, time, strike, and alarm, spring driven; 14" wide, 22" high; **$400.**

E. N. Welch "Beehive Model" rosewood shelf clock; 8-day, time and strike, spring driven; $10\frac{1}{2}$" wide, 19" high, 6" dial; **$300.**

New Haven walnut shelf clock, circa 1865–70; 30-hour, time, strike, and alarm (with key wind on dial and set by the number of hours a person wants to sleep), spring driven; $12\frac{1}{2}$" wide, 22" high; **$275.**

Ansonia walnut shelf clock with imitation mercury pendulum; 8-day, time and strike, spring driven; 12" wide, 22" high; **$225.** *New Haven walnut shelf clock; 8-day, time and strike, spring driven; 14" wide, 23" high;* **$200.**

Ansonia "Berkeley" walnut shelf clock, with notation on label, "Prize medal awarded at the Paris Exposition, 1878"; 8-day, time and strike, spring driven; 15½" wide, 22½" high; **$175.**

W. L. Gilbert walnut-strained shelf clock; 8-day, time, strike, and alarm, spring driven; 13½" wide, 20" high; **$175.**

Ansonia walnut shelf clock; 8-day, time and strike, spring driven; 14" wide, 22" high; **$175.** *W. L. Gilbert mahogany round-top shelf clock, circa 1875; 8-day, time and strike, spring driven; 10¼" wide, 17¾" high;* **$175.**

E. N. Welch walnut shelf clock; 8-day, time and strike, spring driven; 15" wide, 23" high; **$200.**

Seth Thomas "Garfield" walnut shelf clock; 8-day, time and strike, weight driven; 15½" wide, 30" high, 8" dial; **$700.**

E. N. Welch walnut shelf clock, circa 1880; 8-day, time and strike, spring driven; 13½" wide, 23" high, 5" dial; **$325.**

Seth Thomas "Chicago" walnut and mahogany round-top shelf clock, circa 1875; 8-day, time and strike, spring driven; 10½" wide, 17½" high; **$335.**

W. L. Gilbert "Occident" oak shelf clock with walnut panels, made for Columbian Exposition, 1893, mirror sides and replaced brass figures; 8-day, time and strike, spring driven; 16" wide, 23½" high; **$500.**

Closeup of pendulum from W. L. Gilbert "Occident" oak shelf clock.

W. L. Gilbert "Pandia" walnut shelf clock; 8-day, time, strike, and alarm, spring driven; 14" wide, 22" high, 5" dial; **$250.** *W. L. Gilbert "Keystone" rosewood shelf clock; 8-day, time and strike, spring driven; 12½" wide, 18" high;* **$250.**

107

Ansonia "Fifth Avenue" walnut shelf clock; 8-day, time and strike, spring driven; 17" wide, 25" high, 5" dial; **$300.** *American Clock Company "Parlor" walnut shelf clock; 8-day, time and strike, spring driven; 15" wide, 24½" high, 5" dial;* **$500.**

W. L. Gilbert "Walnut Crown" walnut shelf clock; 8-day, time and strike, spring driven; 14" wide, 20" high; **$200.** *E. Ingraham rosewood round-top shelf clock; 8-day, time and strike, spring driven; 11" wide, 18" high;* **$200.**

Ansonia "Britannic" walnut shelf clock, patented June 13, 1882; 30-hour, time and strike; 11" wide, 19½" high, 6" dial; **$125.** *W. L. Gilbert rosewood-veneered shelf clock, circa 1870–80; 8-day, time, bell strike, and alarm;* **$165.**

W. L. Gilbert "Medea" walnut shelf clock; 8-day, time, strike, and alarm, spring driven; 13" wide, 20" high, 5" dial; **$235.** *E. Ingraham walnut shelf clock; 8-day, time, strike, and alarm; 16" wide, 24" high, 5" dial;* **$235.**

E. N. Welch "Judic" (from Patti Series) walnut shelf clock, circa 1890; 8-day, time and strike, spring driven; 12" wide, 20" high, 5" dial; **$800.** *E. N. Welch "Scalchi" (from Patti Series) walnut shelf clock, circa 1875; 8-day, time and strike, spring driven; 12" wide, 20" high, 5" dial;* **$800.**

Ansonia walnut shelf clock with side mirrors and metal figures; 8-day, time, strike, and alarm, spring driven; 14" wide, 21½" high, 5" dial; **$500.** *W. L. Gilbert walnut shelf clock; 8-day, time, strike, and alarm, spring driven; 14" wide, 20½" high;* **$250.**

Sessions mahogany round-top shelf clock, circa 1930; 8-day, time and strike, spring driven; 9" wide, 11" high; **$75.** *Waterbury mahogany round-top shelf clock, circa 1930; 8-day, time and strike, spring driven; 9" wide, 11½" high;* **$75.**

E. Ingraham oak shelf clock; 8-day, time and strike, spring driven; 14¾" wide, 22" high; **$125.** *Ansonia "Beaver" walnut shelf clock with notation on label, "Prize medal awarded Paris Exposition, 1878"; 8-day, time and strike, spring driven; 14½" wide, 23½" high;* **$175.**

Ansonia oak shelf clock with mirror sides and metal figures, circa 1880; 8-day, time and strike, spring driven; 16½" wide, 24" high, 5" dial; **$400.** *W. L. Gilbert walnut simple calendar shelf clock with mirror sides and metal figures; 8-day, time and strike, spring driven; 16½" wide, 24" high, 5" dial;* **$500.** *Notice the similarity between these two cases attributed to different clockmakers.*

E. N. Welch walnut shelf clock; 8-day, time and strike, spring driven; 17" wide, 28½" high, 5" dial; **$300.** *E. N. Welch walnut shelf clock; 8-day, time and strike, spring driven; 14" wide, 28" high, 5" dial;* **$300.**

W. L. Gilbert "Dacca" walnut shelf clock, circa 1880; 8-day, time and strike, spring driven; 12" wide, 21½" high, 5" dial; **$200.** *W. L. Gilbert "Nebo" walnut shelf clock, circa 1880; 8-day, time, strike, and alarm, spring driven; 11½" wide, 22" high, 5" dial;* **$200.**

E. N. Welch "Gerster, V. P." (from Patti Series) walnut shelf clock, circa 1890; 8-day, time and strike, spring driven; 12" wide, 20" high, 5" dial; $800.

Seth Thomas mahogany beehive shelf clock; 8-day, time and Westminster chimes, spring driven; 10" wide, 15" high; $690.

W. L. Gilbert mantel clock with artificially grained wooden case and brass bell on top that rings every half hour, circa 1880; 8-day, time and strike, spring driven; 17" wide, 17½" high; $225.

Seth Thomas "Sonora" chime, 8-bell mahogany shelf clock with inlay; 8-day, time and strike, spring driven; 10" wide, 14" high; no price available.

113

W. L. Gilbert "Forest" walnut shelf clock; 8-day, time, strike, and alarm, spring driven; 16" wide, 25" high; **$300.** *Ansonia "Monarch" walnut shelf clock; 8-day, time and strike, spring driven; 15½" wide, 25" high;* **$400.**

E. Ingraham "Grecian" zebrawood-veneered shelf clock, circa 1880; 30-hour, time and strike, spring driven; 10" wide, 14½" high, 6" dial; **$250.**

Oak Shelf Clocks

George B. Owen oak shelf clock, patented June 17, 1862; time and strike, spring driven; 8" wide; 10¼" high; **$125.**

Ansonia oak shelf clock, dated 1882; 8-day, time and strike, spring driven; 13½" wide, 14" high, 5" dial; **$230.**

Seth Thomas oak shelf clock, circa 1880–90; 8-day, time, strike, and alarm, spring driven; 14" wide, 23½" high, 5" dial; **$225.** Seth Thomas walnut shelf clock, circa 1880–90; 8-day, time, strike, and alarm, spring driven; 14" wide, 23½" high, 5" dial; **$225.** Notice that both cases are identical with the exception of the glass tablets.

Label from W. L. Gilbert "Lion" oak shelf clock.

W. L. Gilbert "Lion" oak shelf clock, circa 1890; 8-day, time and strike, spring driven; 14" wide, 16" high; **$165.**

E. Ingraham pressed-oak shelf clock, circa 1880; 8-day, time and strike, spring driven; 14½″ wide, 19½″ high, 5½″ dial; **$205.** *Ansonia pressed oak shelf clock, circa 1880; 8-day, time and strike, spring driven; 15″ wide, 24″ high, 5½″ dial;* **$210.**

Waterbury oak shelf clock, circa 1890; 8-day, time and strike, spring driven; 15″ wide, 21″ high; **$195.**

116

Ansonia oak shelf clock, circa 1895; 8-day, time and strike, spring driven; 14" wide, 23½" high; $175.

W. L. Gilbert "Long Branch" oak shelf clock; 8-day, time and strike, spring driven; 15½" wide, 29" high, 7" dial; $600.

Label from W. L. Gilbert "Long Branch" oak shelf clock.

W. L. Gilbert "Navy Number 27" pressed-oak shelf clock, circa 1880; 8-day, time and strike, spring driven; 15" wide, 24" high; $175. E. Ingraham walnut shelf clock, circa 1880; 8-day, time and strike, spring driven; 14½" wide, 21" high; $165.

Label from Ansonia "Preston" oak shelf clock.

Ansonia "Preston" oak shelf clock, with label reading, "Prize medal awarded, Paris Exposition, 1878"; 8-day, time and strike, spring driven; 13½" wide, 14" high, 5" dial; **$175.**

Seth Thomas oak shelf clock; 8-day, time, strike, and alarm, spring driven; 15" wide, 25½" high; **$150.**

Closeup of works from Ansonia "Preston" oak shelf clock showing patent, June 18, 1882.

Historical Motif Clocks

E. Ingraham "Admiral Dewey" pressed-oak shelf clock, circa 1899–1905; 8-day, time, strike, and alarm, spring driven; 15" wide, 23" high, 5" dial; **$300.** *E. Ingraham "President McKinley" pressed oak shelf clock, circa 1899–1905; 8-day, time and strike, spring driven; 15" wide, 23" high; 5" dial;* **$300.**

Waterbury "Admiral Dewey" metal shelf clock; 8" wide, 10" high; **$195.**

E. N. Welch "Admiral Schley" pressed-oak shelf clock with the ship "Olympia" on the tablet, circa 1900; 8-day, time and strike, spring driven; 15½" wide, 24" high, 5" dial; **$300.** *Seth Thomas "Fleet Number 2" oak shelf clock with Teddy Roosevelt's four battleships that he sent around the world on a peace cruise pictured on the tablet; 8-day, time and strike, spring driven; 15" wide, 24" high, 5" dial;* **$300.**

Label from Seth Thomas "Fleet Number 2" oak shelf clock.

Closeup of four battleships pictured on tablet of Seth Thomas "Fleet Number 2" oak shelf clock.

Closeup of "Olympia" pictured on tablet of E. N. Welch "Admiral Schley" pressed-oak shelf clock.

E. Ingraham "F.D.R. The Man of the Hour" metal electric shelf clock, circa 1940; 9" wide, 14" high; $70.

E. Ingraham pressed-oak simple calendar shelf clock from the River Series with a ship on the tablet, circa 1905; 8-day, time and strike, spring driven; 15" wide, 23" high, 5" dial; $300. E. Ingraham "Liberty" walnut shelf clock; 8-day, time, strike, and alarm, spring driven; 14½" wide, 23" high, 5" dial; $300.

Black Mantel Clocks

Seth Thomas wooden case, adamantine mantel clock to resemble ebony with marbleized trim, patented September 7, 1880; 8-day, time and strike, spring driven;11¼" wide, 11" high; $75. E. Ingraham mantel clock with black-enameled case to resemble ebony, marbleized columns, and dial of brass and porcelain; 8-day, time and strike, spring driven; 16½" wide, 11" high; $75.

Seth Thomas wooden-case mantel clock with celluloid veneer, called adamantine, circa 1902–17; 8-day, time and strike, spring driven; 9" wide, 10" high; $60. Seth Thomas wooden-case mantel clock with celluloid veneer, called adamantine, circa 1902–17; 8-day, time and strike, spring driven; 8½" wide, 11" high; $60.

Sessions black-enameled wooden-case mantel clock with marbleized trim and brass dial, circa 1910–20; 8-day, time and strike, spring driven; 17" wide, 11" high; **$95.**

Waterbury artificially grained wooden mantel clock with marbleized columns and gilted decorations; 8-day, time and strike, spring driven; 16" wide, 10½" high; **$75.** *New Haven black-enameled wooden mantel clock with marbleized edging and gilted decorations; 8-day, time and strike, spring driven; 11" wide, 12" high;* **$75.**

E. Ingraham black-enameled wooden-case mantel clock with marbleized trim and gilted decorations; 8-day, time and strike, spring driven; 18" wide, 11½" high; **$125.**

Sessions black-enameled wooden-case mantel clock with marbleized trim and gilted decorations; 8-day, time and strike, spring driven; 15" wide, 10½" high; **$75.**

*F. Kroeber black-enameled metal mantel clock with porcelain dial; 8-day, time and strike, spring driven; 13" wide; 12" high; **$185.** Seth Thomas "Mercury" marbleized wooden mantel clock with gilted decorations; 8-day, time, with hour and half-hour chimes, spring driven; 13½" wide, 11" high; **$200.***

*New Haven black-enameled metal case mantel clock with open escapement; 8-day, time and strike, spring driven; 14¼" wide, 10" high; **$120.** Ansonia black-enameled metal-case mantel clock with gilted decorations; 8-day, time and strike, spring driven; 12" wide, 10½" high; **$100.***

Ansonia black-enameled metal-case mantel clock with open escapement; 8-day, time and strike, spring driven; 9½" wide, 10½" high; **$175.**

Waterbury iron-front shelf clock with floral and gilted decorations on case, circa 1850; 30-hour, time and strike, spring driven; 12" wide, 16" high, 3½" dial; **$100.**

Closeup of works only from a 30-hour, time and alarm, spring-driven metal-case shelf clock made by The Terry Clock Company, Waterbury, Connecticut, patented December 1, 1868.

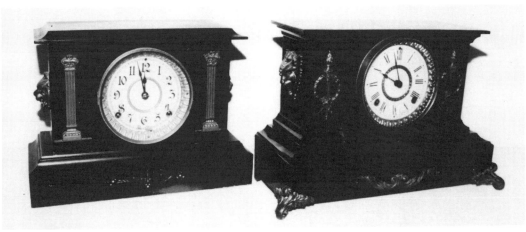

Ansonia black-enameled metal-case mantel clock with gilted decorations; 8-day, time and strike, spring driven; 14" wide, 10" high; **$100.** *Ansonia black-enameled metal-case mantel clock with gilted decorations; 8-day, time and strike, spring driven; 16½" wide, 10½" high;* **$100.**

New Haven black-enameled metal-case mantel clock with applied gilted decorations; 8-day, time and strike, spring driven; 10" wide, 11" high; **$185.** *Unknown maker, black-enameled metal-case mantel clock with marbleized edging; 8-day, time only, spring driven; 8½" wide, 10½" high;* **$185.**

Metal and Iron-Front Clocks

Parker Clock Company, Meriden, Connecticut, solid brass, wooden-base barrel shelf clock, circa 1870; 8-day, time and strike, double-barrel spring driven; 14" wide, 8½" deep, 10½" high; $250.

E. N. Welch brass-washed shelf clock with open escapement; 30-hour, time only, spring driven; 5" wide, 7" high; $125. E. N. Welch brass-washed shelf clock with lever movement; 30-hour, time only; 6½" wide, 8" high; $125. F. Kroeber brass-washed shelf clock, patented May 28, 1878; 30-hour, time and alarm; 5" wide, 7" high; $125.

New Haven copper-wash metal shelf clock with porcelain dial; 8-day, time only, spring driven; 5" wide, 8" high; **$80.**

Unknown maker, copper-washed metal shelf clock, patented December 15, 1908; 30-hour, time only, spring driven; 6" wide, 9½" high; **$75.**

Jennings Brothers, Bridgeport, Connecticut, gilted metal shelf clock (back left) with cherub decoration on top and porcelain dial, patented 1891; 30-hour, time only, spring driven; 4½" wide, 6¼" high; **$125.** *Unknown maker, black metal shelf clock (back right) with porcelain dial; 30-hour, time only, spring driven; 3½" wide, 5" high;* **$125.** *Waterbury gilted metal shelf clock (front) with tin-can movement; 30-hour, time only, spring driven; 8" wide, 10" high;* **$125.**

Jennings Brothers, Bridgeport, Connecticut, metal shelf clock with porcelain dial; 30-hour, time only, spring driven; 6" wide, 13" high; **$150.** *Regent Manufacturing Company, Chicago, metal shelf clock with tin-can movement; 30-hour, time only, spring driven; 11" wide, 12" high;* **$75.**

A. L. Swift, Chicago, metal stove-top clock; 30-hour, time only, spring driven; 8" wide, 10" high; **$75.** *Ansonia iron-front shelf clock, circa 1880; 8-day, time only, spring driven; 10½" wide, 12½" high;* **$150.**

Alarm Clocks

Lux metal shelf clock; 30-hour, time only, spring driven; 4½" wide, 5½" high; **$35.**

Seth Thomas iron-case shelf clock with brass face, dated January 25, 1898; 8-day, time, strike, and alarm, spring driven; 8½" wide, 10" high; **$90.**

Ansonia brass-finished metal shelf clock with cherub figure on top, circa 1884; 30-hour, time and strike, spring driven; 7½" wide, 13" high; **$225.**

Darche Manufacturing Company, Chicago, metal bank (marked "Fireproof, Safety Deposit") shelf clock, patented July 12, 1910; 30-hour, time and alarm; 13" wide, 6" deep, 8" high; **$125.**

Westclox "Ironclad" metal shelf clock; 30-hour, time and alarm, spring driven; 4¼" wide, 5¼" high; **$35.** *USN MD metal shelf clock; 30-hour, time and alarm, 2¾" high;* **$35.** *Ansonia "The Plato" metal digital shelf clock, patented July 7, 1908; 30-hour, time only; 4½" high;* **$150.** *Ansonia "Square Rascal" metal shelf clock; 30-hour, time and alarm; 2¼" wide, 2¾" high;* **$35.**

"Radium" alarm clock, patented December 31, 1912; **$35.** *W. L. Gilbert alarm clock, patented February 16, 1904;* **$35.** *Ansonia "Simplex Automatic" alarm clock, patented November 14, 1914;* **$35.** *The National Call alarm clock with luminous dial and hands;* **$35.**

E. Ingraham "Victory" alarm clock, early 1900; **$35.** Westclox "Baby Ben" alarm clock, patented 1932; **$35.** Westclox "Big Ben" alarm clock; dated March 1, 1922; **$35.** Westclox "Baby Ben" alarm clock, patented November 9, 1920; **$35.**

Unknown maker, wooden castle shelf clock; 30-hour, time and alarm, spring driven; $7\frac{1}{2}''$ wide, 13" high; **$160.**

Celluloid Clocks

Seth Thomas miniature celluloid-case mantel clock; 30-hour, time only, spring driven; 6¼" wide, 4¼" high; **$35.**

Waterbury shelf clock with copper designs on silver-plated case; 30-hour, time only, spring driven; 4" wide, 3" high; **$55.** *New Haven iron-case shelf clock with brass finish; 30-hour, time only, spring driven; 3" wide, 6" high;* **$85.** *New Haven tusculor case (celluloid) shelf clock, dated December 23, 1918, on base; 30-hour, time only, spring driven; 4" wide, 3½" high;* **$55.**

New Haven celluloid shelf clock; 30-hour, time only, spring driven; 5½" wide, 4" high; $55. New Haven "Junior Tattoo Movement" shelf clock, patented April 7, 1904; 30-hour, time and alarm, spring driven; 3" diameter; $45. Waterbury celluloid shelf clock; 30-hour, time only, spring driven; 5" wide, 4½" high; $55.

Unknown maker, celluloid shelf clock; 30-hour, time only, spring driven; 4" wide, 4½" high; $55. Unknown maker, green celluloid shelf clock, with pearl and rhinestone jeweled case; 6½" wide, 3½" high; $85.

6
Novelty Clocks

Did You Know?

The flying pendulum ("Ignatz") clock was advertised as "The best show window attraction ever made. Will draw a crowd wherever exhibited." A ball on a string serves as a pendulum. It swings from side to side and winds and unwinds around two outer posts. The clock was produced about 1883 by the New Haven Clock Company and was called "The craziest clock in the world."

The Lux Clock Manufacturing Company made many wall and shelf novelty clocks. The company, located in Waterbury, Connecticut, was founded in 1917. Current events and comic characters were often the source for their animated clocks. The names De Luxe and a distributor, Keebler, may be found on some of the clocks.

A compressed molded wood was used in the manufacture of many of the Lux clocks. Some were plastic and others were a synthetic marble called "marblesque" with a "wax finish and antiqued" appearance.

Ansonia "Swinging Doll" (moves back and forth as pendulum) shelf clock; 30-hour, time only, spring driven; 7" wide, 8" high; **$550.**

The Ansonia "Bobby Doll" moves up and down to serve as a pendulum. The Ansonia "Swinging Doll" moves back and forth.

New Haven manufactured (with Jerome & Company's name) "Ignatz" (flying pendulum) shelf clock, with A. C. Clausen October 9, 1883, patent movement; 30-hour, time only, hair-spring driven; 7" wide, 10½" high; $300. E. N. Welch "Briggs Rotary" shelf clock with glass dome, patented by John C. Briggs in 1855; 30-hour, time only, spring driven; 7½" high; $450.

Two-Timers were clocks that had a dual function. For example, J. J. Davis, or Davies (sources differ on spelling), patented an illuminated alarm clock around 1877. When the alarm went off, a match lit a lamp. Other two-timer clocks included time clocks, cigar cutters, a pool-room timer, and a cannery clock.

The value of the "Sally Rand" Lux wall clock has increased because the pendulum mentions the Century of Progress, the 1933 World's Fair held in Chicago. This catches the interest of fans of fair memorabilia as well as the attention of clock collectors.

Ansonia "Bobbing Doll" (moves up and down as pendulum) metal shelf clock, patented December 14, 1886, 30-hour, time only, spring driven; 14¾" high; no price available.

Art Deco (or Art Moderne) articles were made in the late 1920s and 1930s. Cubist and geometric forms, step designs, greyhounds, or anything that indicated speed were used as decoration. Interest revived in this art form in the late 1960s.

Wall Clocks

New Haven brass hanging clock with porcelain shield numbers on brass dial, circa 1885; 30-hour, time only, double-spring driven; 15″ diameter; **$350.**

New Haven brass wall clock, circa 1875; 30-day, time only, marine movement with two main-spring drive and balance-wheel control; 8″ diameter; **$375.**

F. Kroeber "Picture Frame" walnut wall clock with velvet backing and key winds hidden under bezel; 8-day, time and strike, spring driven; 11″ wide, 13″ high; **$400.**

*H. J. Davies milk-glass wall clocks, circa 1871–74; 30-hour, time only, spring-driven; left clock 4"
diameter; right clock 5" wide, 7" high;* **$125** *each.*

*Ansonia plush velvet wall clock with brass dec-
orations and porcelain shield numbers on brass
dial; 8-day, time only, two-spring driven; 16" diameter;* **$400.**

Lux Wall Clocks

Lux "Sally Rand" wall clock, with "Century of Progress 1933" on pendulum; 30-hour, time only, spring driven; $200. Lux "Christmas Wreath" wall clock; 30-hour, time only, spring driven; purchased at auction for $1,500. Westclox plastic calico horse wall clock; 30-hour, time only, spring driven; $125.

Lux "Dog on a Fence" and "Cat on a Fence" pendulette wall clocks; 30-hour, time only, spring driven; $275 each. Lux "Fort Dearborn" wall clock with "1933 Century of Progress" on pendulum; 30-hour, time only, spring driven; $425.

Lux "Picaninny" wall clock; **$350.** *"Three Scotties" wall clock;* **$125.** *"Hungry Dog" wall clock;* **$250.** *All are 30-hour, time only, spring-driven pendulettes.*

Lux "Shmoo," **$100.** *Lux "Honey Bunny,"* **$150.** *Lux "Woody Woodpecker,"* **$125.** *All are pendulette wall clocks, 30-hour, time only, and spring driven.*

Lux composition wall clocks, Jack & Jill, Pussy in the Well and Mary Had A Little Lamb; 30-hour, time only, spring driven; **$400** *each.*

Lux "Dog House," **$225.** *Lux "Liberty Bell,"* **$200.** *Lux "Bull Dog,"* **$600.** *All are pendulette wall clocks, 30-hour, time only, and spring driven.*

Lux "Potted Petunia," **$225.** *Lux "Sunflower,"* **$125.** *Lux "Clown with Tie,"* **$400.** *All are pendulette wall clocks, 30-hour, time only, and spring driven.*

Lux "Boy Scout," **$350.** *Lux "Capitol" clock with FDR on top,* **$300.** *Lux "ABC kiddy,"* **$250.** *All are pendulette wall clocks, 30-hour, time only, and spring driven.*

Lux "Golfer," $300. Lux "Country Scene," $300. Lux "Niagara," $300. All are metal pendulette wall clocks, 30-hour, time only, and spring driven.

Lux oak leaf; 10" wide, 19" high; $150. Lux deer head; 10" wide, 19" high; $150. Lux single bird facing left; 9" wide, 17" high; $85. Lux single bird facing right; 7" wide, 15" high; $85. All are molded wood cuckoo pendulette wall clocks, 30-hour, time only, and spring driven.

Lux molded wood pendulette wall clocks with cuckoo clocks at each end; 30-hour, time only, spring driven; 6" wide, 13" to 15" high; **$75** *each.*

Shelf Clocks

Ansonia metal shelf clock with female figures at each corner; 30-hour, time only, spring driven; 5¼" wide, 6" high; **$200.** *Golden Manufacturing Company, Chicago, copper-washed metal case with works by Waterbury, patented 1891; 30-hour, time only, spring driven; 7" high;* **$125.** *Seth Thomas "Shakespeare Bust" gilted metal shelf clock with porcelain dial; 30-hour, time only, spring driven; 4" wide, 8" high;* **$125.**

Western Clock Company, La Salle, Illinois "Volunteers" metal shelf clock, showing two men by a thirteen-star flag; 30-hour, time only, spring driven; 10" high; $100. Western Clock Company gilted metal shelf clock with cherub and grotesque figures, patented October 22, 1902; 30-hour, time only, spring driven; 11" high; $50. Ansonia "Croquet Players" metal shelf clock, patented April 23, 1878; 30-hour, time only, spring driven; 8" wide, 7½" high; $150. Hawkeye Clock Company, Muscatine, Iowa, brass clock and timer combination; 4¾" wide, 6" high; $75.

Triple-towered mahogany cathedral clock, not signed but similar to the handcrafted work of Frank L. & Joseph C. Bily, Spillville, Iowa; 8-day, time only, Lieben marine movement; 19" wide, 11" deep, 36" high; $1,000.

E. N. Welch skeleton shelf clock with glass dome, late 1800; 8-day, time and strike, spring driven; 9¼" diameter, 16" high; no price available.

The Nasco lighter 18-karat gold-plated pocket clock; 1½" wide, 2" high; $40.

Yale Clock Company metal shelf clock, patented 1881; 30-hour, time only, spring driven; 2" wide, 3" high; **$125.** *Parker & Whipple Company metal shelf clock with porcelain dial; 30-hour, time only, spring driven; 4½" wide, 6½" high;* **$100.** *Parker & Whipple Company metal shelf clock; 30-hour, time only, spring driven; 2" wide, 3" high;* **$125.** *Parker & Whipple Company metal shelf clock, patented January 20, 1880; 30-hour, time only, spring driven; 2½" wide, 3" high;* **$125.**

E. N. Welch metal-suitcase shelf clock; 30-hour, time only, spring driven; 3" wide, 2¼" high; **$175.** *New Haven "Tip Top Traveler" metal shelf clock; 30-hour, time only, spring driven; 1¾" high;* **$75.** *New Haven photo-easel shelf clock; 30-hour, time only, spring driven; 5¾" wide, 8" high;* **$100.** *Waterbury miniature brass carriage clock, marked "W. A. Fraser Co., Grain, Chicago"; 30-hour, time only, spring driven; 2" wide, 2½" high;* **$250.**

Two-Timers

Ansonia Brass & Copper Company illuminated alarm clock operates so that match lights lamp when the alarm, patented by H. J. Davis, is tripped; 7½" wide, 17" high; **$1,800.** *Waterbury-movement black-enameled slot-machine mantel clock, early 1900s; the slot machine was patented in 1908 by Loheide Manufacturing Company and was intended to take $2.50 gold pieces; 14" wide, 10½" high;* **$300.**

International Business Machine Corporation time clock, patented March 7, 1916; 22" deep, 35" high; **$700.**

New Haven cannery process clock with "Ayars Machine Company, New Salem, New Jersey," on dial; 15-day, two-spring movement; 18" wide, 39" high; **$400.**

Darche Manufacturing Company, Chicago, wooden-case pool-room timer, circa 1920–30; 8-day, time only, spring driven; 13½" wide, 12" high; **$50.**

150

Barnes Smith & Company cigar cutter with attached unknown-maker clock that is marked "Yale & Co. Jewelers" on dial; 30-hour, time only, spring driven; 14" high; **$300.** *J. Becker & Son "Bonny Jean" cigar cutter with clock movement;* **$100.** *King Alfred Cigar cutter with attached Waterbury clock; 30-hour, time only, spring driven; 13" high;* **$300.**

Lux and Other Later Shelf Clocks

Western Clock Company, La Salle, Illinois, metal horseshoe on wooden-base shelf clock; 30-hour, time only, spring driven; 7½" high; **$200.** *Lux "Rotary Calendar Clock," patented 1932; 5" diameter, 5" high;* **$100.** *E. N. Welch brass shelf clock with open escapement, patented October 1, 1878; 30-hour, time only, spring driven; 7" wide, 8" high;* **$150.**

Lux "The Village Mill" composition shelf clock; 30-hour, time only, spring driven; 8" wide, 10½" high; **$35.** N. Muller's Sons "A Narrow Escape" shelf clock with a cat and mouse on slate, circa 1887; 30-hour, time only, spring driven; 6¾" wide, 8½" high; **$250.**

Lux shelf clock with windmill on celluloid dial, 30-hour, time only, spring driven; 4½" wide, 5½" high; **$125.** Lux shelf clock with Capitol clipper ship on celluloid dial; 30-hour, time only, spring driven; **$125.**

Lux metal shelf clock; 30-hour, time only, spring driven; 1¾" dial; **$35.** Lux sailboat shelf clock; 30-hour, time only, spring driven; 8" wide, 10" high; **$35.** Lux "Louis XVI Art Clock"; 30-hour, time only, spring driven; 1¾" dial; **$35.** Lux "The Homestead" composition shelf clock, pictured in 1927 Sears catalog; 30-hour, time only, spring driven; 10" wide, 6" high; **$35.**

Lux synthetic marble red elephant shelf clock; 30-hour, time only, spring driven; 7" wide, 6½" high, **$125.** Lux synthetic marble white elephant shelf clock; 30-hour, time only, spring driven; 7" wide, 6½" high; **$125.** Ansonia metal elephant shelf clock; 30-hour, time only, spring driven; 9" wide, 9" high; **$125.** Waterbury metal elephant shelf clock; 30-hour, time only, spring driven; 6½" wide, 5½" high; **$125.**

Lux composition cat and owl shelf clocks; 30-hour, time only, spring driven; 5½" high; **$100** each. The Lux composition thermometer, 6" high, is not a clock; **$50.**

Lux Pendulum Stand shelf clocks; 30-hour, time only, spring driven; 5½" to 6½" high; **$125** each.

Lux "The Waiter," "The Drunk," and "The Clown" composition shelf clocks; 30-hour, time only, spring driven; 6½" high; **$75** *each.*

Lux miniature wooden grandfather shelf clock; 30-hour, time only, spring driven; 10½" high; **$65.** *Lux mirror shelf clock; 30-hour, time only, spring driven; 8" square frame;* **$40.** *E. Ingraham miniature wooden grandfather shelf clock; 30-hour, time only, spring driven; 11" high;* **$65.**

DeLux "Bungalow" composition shelf clock, pictured in 1927 Sears catalog; 30-hour, time only, spring driven; 10½" wide, 6" high; **$35.** *W. L. Gilbert miniature wooden round-top shelf clock, patented February 10, 1904; 30-hour, time only, spring driven; 3" wide, 5¼" high;* **$35.** *Lux cast-iron inkwell shelf clock; 30-hour, time only, spring driven; 8" high;* **$200.**

Lux gilted metal shelf clock with man riding horse; 30-hour, time only, spring driven; 4" high; **$75.** *Lux seal and ball metal shelf clock; 30-hour, time only, spring driven; 8" wide, 12" high;* **$100.** *Lux English stirrup shelf clock; 30-hour, time only, spring driven; 5" wide, 5" high;* **$75.** *Waterbury gilted metal shelf clock with buffalo on base; 30-hour, time only, spring driven; 7" high;* **$85.** *Lux bird-in-cage metal shelf clock; 30-hour, time only, spring driven; 5" diameter, 7" high;* **$75.**

Art Deco and Later

Howard Clock Corporation electric "God Bless America" wooden shelf clock, patented 1940; 8½" wide, 8" high; **$225.**

Lux mystery rotary metal shelf clock in Art Moderne black; 5" diameter, 3" high; **$50.**

Unknown maker, metal Art Deco shelf clock; 7" wide, 8½" high; **$55.**

Sessions "Ballerina" electric clock with walnut-stained case and gold-plated figure, patented 1937; 9" wide, 11¼" high; **$65.**

Sessions walnut-veneered electric shelf clock, patented 1936; 20" wide, 19" high; **$37.**

7
Classic Clocks

Did You Know?

Royal Bonn porcelain clock cases were made in Germany, but their works were usually of American manufacture, notably by Ansonia. You cannot assume, however, that a porcelain case is Bonn unless it is marked. Dresden clock cases were also imported from Germany and often contained movements made by American clock manufacturers. They, too, must be labeled in order to be identified as Dresden.

A crystal clock has glass panels on four sides, which expose the works to full view.

Statue Clocks

Ansonia ''Senator'' oak statue shelf clock with brass and silver-plated metal decorations, circa 1880; 8-day, time and strike, spring driven; 15″ wide, 10″ deep, 22″ high, 6″ dial; **$1,500.**

F. Kroeber walnut shelf clock with swinging child pendulum; 8-day, time and strike, spring driven; 12" wide, 20" high, 4½" dial; **$900.** *F. Kroeber statue shelf clock with embossed metal case and metal huntress figure on top; 8-day, time and strike, spring driven; 15" wide, 23" high; 4½" dial;* **$350.**

Label from F. Kroeber metal shelf clock with huntress figure.

Ansonia black-enameled statue shelf clock with bronzed metal decorations, porcelain shield dial numbers and open escapement; 8-day, time and strike, spring driven; 24" wide, 9" deep, 25" high; **$1,500.**

Seth Thomas bronzed metal statue shelf clock with gilted decorations and porcelain dial, distributed by Mitchell Vance & Company, New York; 15-day, time and strike, spring driven; 14" wide, 18" high, 3" dial; no price available.

Ansonia black-enameled metal statue shelf clock with gilted decorations; 8-day, time and strike, spring driven; 13½" wide, 6" deep, 20" high; $350.

Metal statue shelf clock, marked "Sears, Roebuck & Co. Pat. applied for" on back of case; 30-hour, time only, spring driven; 8" wide, 9½" high; $95.

W. L. Gilbert metal statue shelf clock with black-enameled wooden base; 8-day, time and strike, spring driven; 15" wide, 6" deep, 14½" high; $235.

Waterbury metal statue shelf clock with cupid playing the violin, circa 1890; 30-hour, time only, spring driven; 12" high; **$100.** *Waterbury metal statue shelf clock with lady and child figures, patented 1896; 30-hour, time only, spring driven; 5½" wide, 8" high;* **$100.** *New Haven metal statue shelf clock with male child figure; 30-hour, time and strike, spring driven; 6" wide, 10½" high;* **$100.**

Ansonia "Lady with Peacock" black-enameled-base statue shelf clock with porcelain dial and open escapement, circa 1900; 8-day, time and strike, spring driven; 21" wide, 8½" deep, 19½" high; **$800.**

Crystal Clocks

Seth Thomas "Empire Number 10" crystal regulator shelf clock, circa 1900; 8-day, time and strike, spring driven; 8" wide, 6½" deep, 14½" high; **$425.**

Ansonia "Floral" crystal regulator gold-finish (catalogue description) shelf clock, with porcelain dial and open escapement; 8-day, time and strike, spring driven; 9" wide, 8" deep, 16" high; **$1,100.**

Ansonia "Regal" crystal regulator shelf clock, with porcelain dial and open escapement; 8-day, time and strike, spring driven; 10½" wide, 9" deep, 19" high; **$2,600.**

Davies "Crystal Gem" mirror-back shelf clock, patented March 23, 1875; 8-day, time and strike, spring driven; 16" high; $400. Davies wooden-case shelf clock with warrior head on pendulum; 8-day, time and strike, spring driven; 16" high; $400.

Label from Davies "Crystal Gem" shelf clock.

Porcelain Clocks

Unknown maker, shelf clock with Jasperware case; 30-hour, time only, spring driven; 4½" wide, 6" high; $100. New Haven porcelain shelf clock with Van Dyke painting on case; 30-hour, time only, spring driven; 4" wide, 7" high; $100. Waterbury porcelain shelf clock with floral design on case; 30-hour, time only, spring driven; 4" wide, 6" high; $100. New Haven shelf clock with Jasperware case; 30-hour, time only, spring driven; 5½" wide, 7" high; $100.

Ansonia Royal Bonn porcelain shelf clock with floral decorations on white case, circa 1890; 8-day, time and strike, spring driven; 10" wide, 12" high; **$465.** *F. Kroeber porcelain shelf clock with cobalt blue, gilt, and floral decorated case, circa 1890; 8-day, time and strike, spring driven; 9" wide, 14" high;* **$675.** *W. L. Gilbert porcelain shelf clock with floral decorations on pale green case, circa 1890; 8-day, time and strike, spring driven; 9" wide, 10½" high;* **$445.**

New Haven porcelain small-case shelf clock; 30-hour, time only, spring driven; 6" wide, 5" high; **$55.**

New Haven shelf clock with Jasperware case; 30-hour, time only, spring driven; 4¼" wide, 6" high; **$125.** *New Haven shelf clock with windmill painting on porcelain case; 30-hour, time only, spring driven; 4¼" wide, 9¼" high;* **$125.** *New Haven shelf clock with Jasperware case; 30-hour, time only, spring driven; 4" wide, 5" high;* **$150.** *New Haven Delft porcelain shelf clock; 4½" wide, 7¾" high;* **$150.**

Ansonia porcelain shelf clock with blue and gold decorated case, patented June 18, 1882, by Tuckahoe China; 8-day, time and strike, spring driven; 9" wide, 11" high; $235. Ansonia Royal Bonn porcelain case; 8-day, time and strike, spring driven; 9½" wide, 11¼" high; $210. Ansonia ''Tally'' porcelain shelf clock, circa 1900; 8-day, time and strike, spring driven; 9¼" wide, 10¼" high; $295.

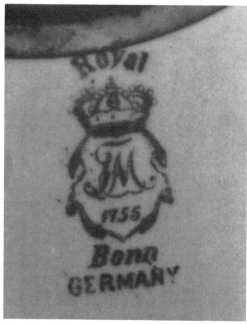

Closeup of Royal Bonn, Germany, mark on porcelain shelf clock.

Ansonia Dresden porcelain shelf clock; 8-day, time and strike, spring driven; 13" wide, 12" high, 4½" dial; $350.

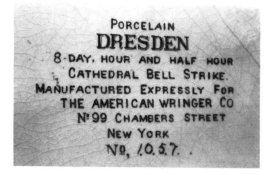

PORCELAIN
DRESDEN
8-DAY, HOUR AND HALF HOUR
CATHEDRAL BELL STRIKE.
MANUFACTURED EXPRESSLY FOR
THE AMERICAN WRINGER CO
Nº 99 CHAMBERS STREET
NEW YORK
Nº. 10.5.7.

Label from Ansonia Dresden porcelain shelf clock.

New Haven "San Remo" porcelain wall clock, 1-day, time only, hair-spring driven; 9" wide, 10" high, 2½" dial; **$175.**

New Haven porcelain wall clock; 1-day, time only, hair-spring driven; 7" wide, 8" high, 1¾" dial; **$150.**

Ansonia Royal Bonn porcelain shelf clock, with porcelain dial and open escapement; 8-day, time and strike, spring driven; 10½" wide, 11½" high; **$600.**

Ansonia Royal Bonn porcelain small-case shelf clock with floral decorations; 8-day, time and strike, spring driven; 7½" wide, 7" high. **$250.**

8
A Vintage "Grandfather" and the Timely Tale of an Exact Copy

Did You Know?

"Floor clock," "tall-case," or "long-case" clock are terms that refer to what is now called a "grandfather" clock. Clockmakers in this country crafted them between 1700 and 1840. The title "grandfather" clock likely was applied after 1876, when a song about "My Grandfather's Clock" was popular. It was a floor clock, too tall for a shelf.

A regulator clock traditionally is an accurate clock with a precise mechanism. Railroad depots used them to make sure trains ran on schedule. Jewelry stores frequently had one in the window. It helped advertise the store and allowed passersby to set their watches by its exact time. Clock and watch repairers could be sure a timepiece was functioning properly by checking it against the regulator. The term lost its meaning when the word "regulator" began to be used too freely on too many clocks.

Early clockmakers were inventive men. Some collectors today share that trait. One man preserves history by making new, exact-copy cases for old movements. He wants everything to be precisely like the original and uses a pocketknife to hand-carve pieces from the old wood he salvages, retrieved perhaps from discarded furniture. He never begins a project until he has pictures and all the necessary measurements. If he needs large pieces of wood, he will cut down a tree of the desired species and have the wood kiln-dried so that his clock will be authentic.

Pictured is an exact copy of a jeweler's regulator created from wood from an oak tree the craftsman cut down and had kiln-dried. He measured the old clock so precisely that "you could take the door off mine and switch it with theirs and it would match perfectly," he explained.

Waterbury oak jeweler's regulator floor clock; 8-day, time only, weight driven; 31" wide, 13" deep, 105¼" high; **$2,500** *for exact copy;* **$5,000** *for original clock.*

Ithaca oak floor clock (grandfather clock), circa 1920; 8-day, time and strike, spring driven; 18" wide, 11" deep, 82" high; **$600.**

The original Waterbury jeweler's regulator, a floor clock, has a dead-beat escapement, a sweep second hand, and is 8-day and weight driven. The reproduction has the same features, with only one difference: so as not to waste space, the craftsman made a storage unit in the base of his exact copy.

Glossary

Acorn clock: A clock whose shape resembles that of an acorn.

Adamantine: A patented colored celluloid applied as veneer.

Advertising clock: A clock used for promotional purposes on which the advertising may be found on the case, dial, or tablet.

Alarm: An attachment that rings or gongs at a preselected time.

Animated clock: A clock that incorporates a lifelike movement characteristic of an animal or person.

Anniversary clock: A clock that runs for a full year. Sometimes called a 400-day clock; it is wound annually.

Apron: A decorative piece, sometimes used to hide construction details. It may be on the bottom of a case or between the legs of a floor or shelf clock.

Arabic numerals: Figures on a dial written 1, 2, 3, etc.

Arc: The swinging path of a clock pendulum.

Backboard: The inside back of a clock case where a label frequently was applied.

Balance: The oscillating wheel that, along with the hair-spring, regulates the speed of a clock.

Banjo clock: The name given to Simon Willard's "Improved Timepiece," a wall clock, because of its shape.

Beading: A type of carved or applied molding.

Beat: The ticking sound of a clock. When the ticking is consistently steady, it is "in beat." If it is irregular, it is "out of beat."

Beehive clock: A clock with a rounded case that bears some resemblance to a beehive.

Bevel: A chamfer such as the angled edge on plate glass.

Bezel: A ring of wood or metal that surrounds and holds the glass over the clock dial.

Black clocks: Clocks made of marble, black iron, or black enameled wood, popular from about 1880 to 1920.

Bob: The weight at the bottom end of a pendulum rod.

Bracket clock: The British name for a shelf clock.

Brass works: A clock mechanism made of brass.

Calendar clock: A clock that can indicate the day, month, and date, or combinations thereof, as well as the time. A perpetual calendar makes provisions for the various lengths of months and adjusts accordingly, whereas a simple calendar must be changed manually to accommodate a change from a 30-day to a 31-day month.

Case: The housing for the works of a clock.

Celluloid: A trade name for the first artificial plastic, invented in 1869, that received wide commercial use. Some clock cases in the early 1900s were made of this highly flammable material.

Chamfer: A sloping or angled edge on wood or plate glass; a bevel.

China or porcelain clock: A clock with a case made of glazed porcelain.

Clock: A machine that records the passing of time and strikes at least on the hour.

Cornice: The horizontal molded projection at the top of a clock case.

Crystal regulator: A shelf clock with glass panels on all four sides.

Date dial: An additional clock dial that shows the dates of the month.

Dead-beat escapement: A clock escapement that does not recoil (fall back).

Dial: A clock's face with numbers and hands.

Ebonized: A black finish that looks like ebony wood.

Eight-day clock: A clock that runs for eight days on one winding.

Escapement: The clock mechanism that controls the swing of the pendulum or the movement of the balance wheel.

Escutcheon: The trim around a keyhole.

Finial: A wooden or metal spire or turning.

Flying pendulum (also referred to as "Ignatz"): A novelty clock invented in 1883 and made again in the late 1950s. Hanging from an arm, a small ball on a thread swings in a horizontal circle and is regulated by twisting and untwisting around vertical rods on each side of the clock.

Four-hundred-day clock: See *Anniversary clock*.

Frame: The case of a clock.

Fusee or fuzee: A grooved cone upon which the cord from the spring container unwinds to equalize the force of the spring in a clock.

Gallery clock: An 8-day or electric clock with a simple case and a dial usually eight inches or larger that hung on the wall in a public establishment.

Gilt: A gold-colored coating.

Gold leaf: An extremely thin sheet of solid gold sometimes applied as a decoration on columns, tablets, or other parts of a clock case.

Gothic case: A case, a variation of a steeple clock, with a pointed top that bears a resemblance to Gothic architecture.

Grandfather clock: The name for a floor-standing clock in a tall, upright case. Originally called a long-case or tall-case clock.

Grandmother clock: A smaller floor-standing version of a grandfather clock.

Hair-spring: A slender hairlike coil that controls the regular movement of the balance wheel in a clock.

Hands: The time indicators that mark the hours, minutes, or seconds on a clock dial.

Hanging shelf-clock: A wall clock with a shelflike base that makes it appear as if it is sitting on a shelf.

Horology: The science of measuring time or making timepieces.

"Ignatz": See *Flying pendulum*.

Iron-front: A shelf clock with a cast-iron front.

Kidney dial: A dial on a clock that resembles the shape of a kidney.

Kitchen clock: A clock frequently of oak, manufactured from the late 1800s to the early 1900s, that sat on a shelf in the kitchen.

Long-case clock: The original name for a grandfather clock.

Looking-glass clock: A clock with a boxlike case and mirror instead of a painted glass tablet.

Mainspring: The principal or driving power that keeps the mechanism running in a spring-driven clock.

Mantel clock: A shelf clock.

Marine or lever clocks: Clocks that operate with a hair-spring balance and continue to run when transported or set on an uneven surface (contrary to pendulum clocks). Often used aboard ships.

Mask: A human or animal face used as a decoration.

Medallion: An applied circular, oval, or square decorative turning used on a clock case.

Mercury pendulum: In American clocks, a silvery-looking, usually cylindrical pendulum that resembles French examples, which actually contained mercury.

Mirror clock: See *Looking glass*.

Mission style: A straight-lined, plain clock case that was popular from about 1900 to 1925.

Molding: A continuous decorative edging.

Movement: The "works" of a clock.

Novelty clock: A small, often animated clock, usually in the shape of a familiar object.

OG, or ogee: A double, continuous S-like curve used as a molding on certain straight, rectangular clocks of the early 1800s.

Open escapement: The wheel and pallet movement that can be seen on some clock dials.

Pallet: A catching device that regulates the speed of a clock by releasing one notch of a toothed wheel (rachet wheel) at each swing of the pendulum or turn of the balance wheel.

Parlor clock: The older, carved-case, often walnut, Victorian clock of the mid- to late 1800s that stood on a shelf or mantel in the parlor, as opposed to a shelf clock of pressed oak or simpler designed walnut from the 1890s or early 1900s.

Pediment: An ornamental top on a clock case, frequently curved in shape.

Pendulum: A clock weight, often ornamental, hung from a fixed point so as to swing to and fro as it regulates the clock's movement.

Perpetual: See *Calendar clock*.

Regulator clock: Originally a term for an accurate clock.

Reverse painting: A picture or design often used on a clock tablet and painted on the back side of a glass in reverse order of a normal painting.

Roman numerals: Roman letters used as numerals on clock dials, as in I, II, III, IV, etc. On older clocks, four was often represented by IIII, an old Roman numeral for IV. It is said that this form better balances the VIII on the other side of the dial.

Shelf clock: A clock designed to sit on a shelf or mantel.

Simple calendar: See *Calendar clock*.

Spandrels: The four corners, featuring painted designs or metal decorations, that square off a round clock dial.

Spring clock: A clock whose power is provided by springs.

Steeple clock: A clock with a sharply pointed Gothic case and finials at each side.

TP: An abbreviation for timepiece.

T & S: An abbreviation for time and strike.

Tablet: The front, lower glass, frequently painted, on a clock case.

Tall clock: A long-case, floor clock, often called a grandfather clock.

Tambour clock: A shelf clock, also called a humpback or camelback clock, with a case that is flat at each side and rounded in the middle.

Thirty-day clock: A clock that requires winding once a month.

Thirty-hour clock: A clock that runs for thirty hours without rewinding.

Time and strike: A clock that both tells the time and strikes or chimes.

Timepiece: A clock that tells time only and does not strike or chime.

Visible escapement. See *Open escapement*.

Wagon spring: A series of flat springs, attributed to Joseph Ives of Bristol, Connecticut, used instead of a coil spring to power the clock movement.

Wall clock: A clock that hangs on the wall.

Weights: The power source that drives the mechanism in a clock when it is not spring driven.

Zebrawood: An African wood, straw colored with fine stripes, that is sliced into veneers to cover a base wood. Also called *zebrano*.

Bibliography

Bailey, Chris. *Two Hundred Years of American Clocks and Watches.* Englewood Cliffs: A Rutledge Book, Prentice-Hall, no date.

Distin, William H., and Robert Bishop. *The American Clock.* New York: E. P. Dutton, 1976.

Drepperd, Carl W. *American Clocks and Clock Makers.* Garden City: Doubleday & Company, 1947.

Ehrhardt, Roy. *Official Price Guide to Antique Clocks.* Westminster: The House of Collectibles, 1985.

Ehrhardt, Roy, and Red Rabeneck. *Clock Identification and Price Guide.* Kansas City, MO: Heart of America Press, 1983.

Mebane, John. *The Coming Collecting Boom.* New York: A. S. Barnes and Company, 1968.

Miller, Andrew Hayes, and Dalia Marcia Miller. *Survey of American Clocks: Calendar Clocks.* Elgin, IL: Antiquitat, 1972.

Miller, Robert W. *Clock Guide Identification with Prices.* Des Moines: Wallace-Homestead Book Company, 1974.

_____. *Clock Guide No. 2 Identification with Prices.* Des Moines: Wallace-Homestead Book Company, 1975.

_____. *Clock Guide Identification with Prices.* Lombard: Wallace-Homestead Book Company, 1981.

Palmer, Brooks. *The Book of American Clocks*. New York: The Macmillan Company, 1950.

_____. *A Treasury of American Clocks*. New York: The Macmillan Company, 1967.

Schiff, Leonard J., and Joseph L. Schiff. *Edward Payson Baird: Inventor, Industrialist, Entrepreneur*. Plattsburgh, NY: Clinton Press, 1975.

Catalogues

Israel, Fred L., ed. *1897 Sears, Roebuck Catalogue,* New York: Chelsea House Publishers, 1976.

Ly, Tran Duy. *Chelsea Clock Co. Calalog E. 1911*. Arlington: Arlington Horology & Book Co., 1987.

Schroeder, Joseph J., Jr., ed. *1908 Sears, Roebuck Catalogue*. Chicago: The Gun Digest Company, 1969.

Pamphlets

Bulletin of the National Association of Watch and Clock Collectors, Inc. "Eli Terry— Dreamer, Artisan, and Clockmaker." Columbia, PA, Summer 1965.

Miller, Andrew Hayes, and Dalia Marcia Miller. *Illinois Horology: A Brief View into the Land of Lincoln*. Chicago, 1977.

Index

About the Authors

Bob and Harriett Swedberg especially enjoy collecting antiques because of the fine friendships they have made with others who share this interest. This hobby links the generations, binds various nationalities together, and spans economic barriers. The Swedbergs like to share their knowledge through teaching classes, conducting seminars, lecturing, and exhibiting items at antiques shows. They have written columns including "Antique Echoes" in *Collectors Journal* and have been featured guests on many radio and television programs. These Moline, Illinois, residents are available for programs.